AF896212

Palgrave Studies in Economic History

Series Editor
Kent Deng, London School of Economics, London, UK

Palgrave Studies in Economic History is designed to illuminate and enrich our understanding of economies and economic phenomena of the past. The series covers a vast range of topics including financial history, labour history, development economics, commercialisation, urbanisation, industrialisation, modernisation, globalisation, and changes in world economic orders.

Stefan Kirkegaard Sløk-Madsen

Danish Capitalism in the 20th Century

A Business History of an Innovistic Mixed Economy

palgrave
macmillan

Stefan Kirkegaard Sløk-Madsen
Copenhagen Business School
Frederiksberg, Denmark

ISSN 2662-6497 ISSN 2662-6500 (electronic)
Palgrave Studies in Economic History
ISBN 978-3-031-04266-9 ISBN 978-3-031-04267-6 (eBook)
https://doi.org/10.1007/978-3-031-04267-6

JEL Classification Codes: N940 Regional and Urban History: Europe: 1913-; N800 Micro-Business History: General, International, or Comparative; P11 Planning, Coordination, and Reform; Capitalist Systems: Political Economy; O520 Economywide Country Studies: Europe
General Keywords: Denmark; welfare state; capitalism; Business history; Mixed Economy; Institutional Economics; Innovation

© The Editor(s) (if applicable) and The Author(s), under exclusive license to Springer Nature Switzerland AG 2022
This work is subject to copyright. All rights are solely and exclusively licensed by the Publisher, whether the whole or part of the material is concerned, specifically the rights of translation, reprinting, reuse of illustrations, recitation, broadcasting, reproduction on microfilms or in any other physical way, and transmission or information storage and retrieval, electronic adaptation, computer software, or by similar or dissimilar methodology now known or hereafter developed.
The use of general descriptive names, registered names, trademarks, service marks, etc. in this publication does not imply, even in the absence of a specific statement, that such names are exempt from the relevant protective laws and regulations and therefore free for general use.
The publisher, the authors, and the editors are safe to assume that the advice and information in this book are believed to be true and accurate at the date of publication. Neither the publisher nor the authors or the editors give a warranty, expressed or implied, with respect to the material contained herein or for any errors or omissions that may have been made. The publisher remains neutral with regard to jurisdictional claims in published maps and institutional affiliations.

Cover illustration: Holger Burmeister/Alamy Stock Photo

This Palgrave Macmillan imprint is published by the registered company Springer Nature Switzerland AG
The registered company address is: Gewerbestrasse 11, 6330 Cham, Switzerland

Dedicated to my three amazing sons, Ludwig, Conrad, and Ditlev —Ideas matter, trade matters, so never stop either and always give equal liberty and dignity to all humans.

Foreword

Denmark is, like the other Scandinavian countries increasingly seen as an exemplar nation. The country scores highly on democracy, is very low in corruption and very high in generalized trust, and has remarkably, been able to combine high levels of wealth creation and economic freedom with a very large government sector and levels of taxation in the top worldwide.

What is the cause, or causes, of all this? Are the causes perhaps intertwined? If so, what does the web of causes look like? A traditional answer is "factor endowments"; however, Denmark doesn't have obvious natural resources. An updated answer is a "highly educated workforce" and while this is true for Denmark, it is also true for many other countries.

Increasingly, social scientists have been looking to institutional and, broadly, ideological determinants of why countries perform differently. Institutions are the formal and informal rules of the game (including trust), and, as Deirdre McCloskey's work reminds us of, they are strongly intertwined with the generally held beliefs that are manifest in political ideology and also religion. Institutions and ideology tend to evolve slowly over time in cultural evolutionary processes that are still relatively ill-understood. As Nobel Prize laureate Friedrich von Hayek stressed, we follow successful "rules", often without necessarily understanding why they are successful.

However, things like institutions, ideology, rules, and so on are "macro" categories. They shape history to the extent that they influence people's actions (and are themselves changed over time by actions). Also, while institutions and shared beliefs are necessary to the functioning of societies, they may of course also be stifling. The institutions of what Hayek called the "Great Society" (much of the West) with its emphasis on freedom in a number of dimensions, are obviously very different from the institutions that guided the evolution of most other historical societies.

Thus, as Dr. Stefan Sløk-Madsen explains in this book, we need to look beyond factor endowments and institutions, and look at the actual actions of people in the production of wealth, high levels of trust, and so on. Moreover, to understand the current situation, we need to understand how that situation came about from a historical perspective, not the least how entrepreneurs and business people and the companies they founded combined available factors of production to create wealth.

To this end, Dr. Sløk-Madsen very skillfully combines an investigation of Denmark's national and international historical past on the macro level with an inquiry into the business history of the nation. This is a work that is at the same time multidisciplinary, enlisting the disciplines of economics, management research, economics and political science, and multi-level, featuring discussions of individuals, firms, institutions, and societies. It is bold, informative, and enlightening—and highly recommended.

Nicolai J. Foss
Professor
Copenhagen Business School
Frederiksberg, Denmark

Preface

This book is a work of love, but also of necessity. As a Danish social scientist, one is often stuck with wonder when reading about Danish social structures and institutional arrangements and outcomes in international outlets—both academic and popular. Like all countries, Denmark is unique, with a unique historical outcome shaped by the multitude of choices made by the millions of humans who have either directly inhabited the country or have influenced it from outside its borders. What makes Denmark more unique than most is the universal welfare state model, which also earns immense political interest from the right[1] to the left. Danish institutions, or some idealized non-factual version of them, have even been an argument in US Presidential elections.[2] However, it is reasonably challenging for non-Danish speakers to truly understand why Denmark got its present economic shape. Therefore, this book is necessary, as it aims to use mainly Danish language sources to give an accessible yet comprehensive and academic account of a much talked about, yet poorly understood, example of a mixed economy and a prime example of

[1] Most famous recent example is likely the Trish Regan Fox News segment: "Everyone in Denmark is working for the Government". *YouTube* (2018), https://www.youtube.com/watch?v=pSFfTG42Jl8, Accessed Oct 12, 2021.

[2] Jim Tankersley, "Why Bernie Sanders Loves Denmark and Hillary Doesn't", *Washington Post* (2015), https://www.washingtonpost.com/news/wonk/wp/2015/10/13/why-bernie-sanders-loves-denmark-but-hillary-clinton-doesnt/, Accessed Oct 12, 2021.

a universal welfare state. The book relies mostly on academic sources or reports from respected organizations, but includes other sources where necessary. Other sources can be autobiographies, books by journalists, or even debate-oriented works by policymakers and would-be policymakers. That said, the primary works referenced are the growing Danish research literature on the relevant topics. I am, as such, genuinely indebted to many better scholars than me.

Therefore, this book is mainly written for an international audience interested in understanding the Danish economy per se or a case of a mixed economy more generally. That is the main contribution. The second contribution is, as described above, the usage of sources that is hard even to locate, let alone read, for non-Danes. Thirdly, the book is not written by a historian but by an economist, be it one with a deep interest in history and knowledge of historical methods. I am too humble to present new historical evidence in this work—others more skilled than I are better at that. However, I will present historical changes and explanations from a slightly different light using my economics training than some historians might; For instance, I present the conditions that created the Danish welfare state, in a novel way: the Danish welfare state creation as a failed state outcome driven by special interest groups.

As an economist, it is natural to tell Danish Capitalism's history as a business history. It is also an attempt to tell a bottom-up history to as far a degree as possible. As interesting as redistribution and state production might be to some readers, the fact remains that there would be nothing to redistribute without firms and markets generating wealth. Even a casual look at Danish businesses will reveal that longevity is a shared variable and that many firms predate the modern welfare state. There are, therefore, four fundamental and interrelated assumptions behind this book, which help to constitute the underlying research design:

- Firstly, the most internationalized and export-oriented Danish companies tend to be the largest companies founded 50 plus years ago—many before 1945.
- Secondly, a number of the largest Danish companies have been extraordinarily successful in exploiting global niches in particular since the early 1990s.
- Thirdly, these large companies have been marked by peculiar types of ownership, including foundations and cooperatives.

- Fourthly, these successful large companies were engaged in very different industries from a variety of sectors, including food and beverages, shipping, medical industries, fashion, energy, and manufacturing.

The fact that old and large Danish corporations were successful after 1990 across different industries and ownership types lead to a twofold hypothesis of the book: being old and Danish mattered to the globalized companies. This hypothesis leads to the three overall and related research questions:

1. Why did Danish Capitalism foster so different companies that proved globally competitive?
2. How were these companies impacted by—and did they impact—Danish Capitalism?
3. To what degree does the case of Denmark give evidence to innovism—the notion that free development and testing of ideas as opposed to capital access and accumulation or institutional arrangements and stability—is the main explanation for prosperity as observed in modern times?

This book will provide evidence and discuss matters related to these overall research questions in 7 independent chapters and finally revisited, summarized, and answered in the concluding remarks toward the end of this book.

Frederiksberg, Denmark Stefan Kirkegaard Sløk-Madsen

Acknowledgements

When I took social sciences classes in high school, it was a nerdy dream to sometime in the future write a book on Danish society from a historical perspective. As I much—much—later wrote my Ph.D. and was lucky to talk to many international people more skilled, knowledgeable, and intelligent, then I, the realization dawned that while there was a surprisingly high interest in Danish society and modern history, but there was very little knowledge about it internationally. I therefore count myself immensely privileged and lucky that I have been given a chance with this book to both satisfy my old dream, and potentially make an important contribution to international social science. To try to convey such a vast topic as this to an academic audience has been humbling and fun. All mistakes and omissions are—needless to say—mine alone. Yet, I need to thank a number of people, without who this friendly support, this book would not have happened.

This book has been way too long in the making. It was born when my old master thesis supervisor, esteemed business historian and vice dean at Copenhagen Business School Martin Iversen, asked if I wanted to co-write it. Martin unfortunately had to abandon the project, but I am extremely grateful for the opportunity he has given me here. Martin is a wonderful scholar, he, Steen Andersen (my former bachelor thesis supervisor, now at Rigsarkivet), and the amazing Ole Lange have all gone above and beyond as teachers and showed me the amazing power of business history to explain society. I sat out to draft an outline while being a visiting scholar at Sauder School of Business at UBC in 2016. However, it took me a long time to actually write it. I will not bore the reader with the excuses, or even try to sell you on the fact that time matured the project. I will simply say, that I cannot stress how lucky I am to have Ruth Jenner, Uma Vinesh, Srishti Gupta, Ellie Duncan, and the team at Palgrave be so patient. Thank you!

Alfred Marshall was right when he said that all modern economists stand on the shoulders of giants. So do I, in a very real way. This work is in many ways a review of the immense body of research in Danish—I have often found myself in awe at the works cited here. I further simply would never have finished this book without the giant help of my assistant Henrik M. Nielsen. He has been an insightful workhorse who tirelessly supply research and stood for hour-long qualified discussions on the topics of the book. Several ideas in this book owe much to him, and I know he will be an amazing academic historian should he choose to be one. But as with much talent, the choice is his. He should likely excel in almost any venture he will set his sights on.

I am also very thankful toward Professor Nicolai J. Foss, who has been an essential intellectual inspiration for me since I, by chance, found a copy of his 1994 book "The Austrian School and Modern Economics" in my second year of undergrad. As a phenomenal teacher on my master's program—I still remember the toaster slide. All the way to his 2012 book (with Peter Klein) "Organizing Entrepreneurial Judgment: A New Approach to the Firm", which became the intellectual anchor of my Ph.D., as did many of his papers. Those books and many of his papers are classics, in my view, and he is one of the best and most crucial modern management scholars. To have him grace my work with a foreword is a big honor.

Further, I need to thank the scholars who has been kind enough to endorse my work. I am humbled and blessed that such people took the time and showed the patience to read early drafts. It is very inspiring for further work to have such intellectual towers encourage you. Thank you Siri Terjesen Art Carden, Bruce Caldwell, Zoltan Acs, David Iglesias, and Christian Bjørnskov. They are all role models for both their work and the service they do.

Likewise, a big thank you to CEPOS, particularly, the donors and the president Martin Ågerup who have allowed me and supported me in writing this book. CEPOS is such an important and needed organization in Denmark; it is truly amazing to work there. I am especially indebted to a former colleague, Henrik Christoffersen whose initial guidance in this book project has been very important.

Besides my wonderful colleagues at CEPOS who have all helped me immensely to discuss issues and locate references, I also like to thank David Crowther of the History of England Podcast. That podcast is truly an astonishing feat which has given me a lot of joy—it is from him I owe the Alfonsi quote in the Concluding Remarks. I also like to extend a huge thank you to Kamilla Holmgaard from Det Økonomiske Råd for helping supply data. I am very grateful to all the insightful who have taken time to talk to me and who have recommended the project to others. Also, a big thank you to Andelsforeningernes Humanitære og Kulturelle Fond who kindly offered to support expenses for the book. I am very grateful, but just like all others, they have had no say in the content. I am also indebted to Balder Asmussen who is a challenging discussant partner on the formative years of the welfare state and the surrounding economic policy and conditions—his comments has been very helpful indeed. Also, while I did try to track down the ownership rights to the Stjernen ad, I simply was not able. I hope the right owner and artists will forgive my use of their fine work.

Lastly, but most importantly, I must thank my darling patient wife Katja. Without her immense patience and support, this could never have happened. I am sorry I spend so many words on works as these and have so few left for the important matters. Love you!

Praise for *Danish Capitalism in the 20th Century*

"Sløk-Madsen's rich historical narrative is a significant addition to our understanding of the many varieties of capitalism, and a true case study of 'innovism'. The account of Danish firm-based capitalism explores four key and "uncontested" pillars of Denmark's success: freedom of speech, free markets generate wealth, small nation, and socialist compromise. The extensive references, including many Danish language-only sources, dispel the misguided notion held by many non-Danes that Denmark's remarkable success is somehow due to a socialist welfare state. This text is a must-read for any student of Danish economic history, as well as for practitioners and policymakers who will need to understand the historical context and many experiments in order to develop and implement change."

—Siri Terjesen, *Professor of Entrepreneurship & Associate Dean for Research and External Relations at Florida Atlantic University College of Business*

"How does a small country of only six million compete in the global economy? Stefan K. Sløk-Madsen expertly answers that question in his compelling new book, Danish Capitalism in the 20th Century, A Business History of an Innovistic Mixed Economy. Many incorrectly believe Denmark is a socialist state. After reading this book, they will understand that Denmark's economy is clearly capitalistic but implements a high tax rate with comprehensive welfare benefits.

Sløk-Madsen masterfully provides an economic history of Denmark and explains how a small country with no large natural resources was able to create such large globally diverse companies as Maersk, Lego, Bang & Olufsen, and Carlsberg. The Danish penchant for citizen trust in each other, in institutions, property rights and the rule of law coupled with minimal corruption make ideal grounds for an "innovistic" economy or one that focuses on the interaction of traditional institutions and the consensus driven freedom to try novel approaches. While there are many types of capitalism the Danish variant has flourished by using the country's location, size and demographics to its full economic benefit."

—David Iglesias, J. D. Jean and E. Floyd Kvamme, *Associate Professor of Politics and Law and Director of Wheaton Center for Faith, Politics and Economics at Wheaton College*

"Sløk-Madsen traces the institutional changes that accompanied the transition of Denmark from a liberal market economy to a full-blown welfare state. For readers who, like myself, know little about this story, this is the book for you."

—Bruce J. Caldwell, *Research Professor of Economics and Director of Center for the History of Political Economy, Duke University*

"This book is a tour-de-force in the history of Danish capitalism, and the author possess the courage to provide a liberalistic argument. The author promotes the importance of private innovation in contrast to the well-known understanding of Danish capitalism as a state-driven development of a welfare society. The importance of public institutions and welfare is recognized by the author but the point is that economic progress is to be understood in a market economic context driven by individual private entrepreneurs rather than in a welfare context driven by a large public sector. It is a thought-provoking and recommendable read for the domestic as well as the international audience. "Danish Capitalism in the 20th Century – a Business History of an Innovistic Mixed Economy" is based on a solid theoretic understanding of the concept of capitalism and an in-depth analysis of the historical development."

—Martin Jes Iversen, *Associate Professor of Business History and Vice Dean of International Education, Copenhagen Business School*

"This book is a very timely and insightful corrective to the stories often told by media and politicians about Denmark. Stefan K. Sløk-Madsen not only documents how Denmark grew rich before the welfare state, but also how the current welfare state rests on a highly capitalist private sector, and how that sector developed. His book is a must-read to anyone with an interest in the quirks and special features of the Scandinavian societies and their thoroughly individualist market institutions."

—Christian Bjørnskov, *Professor of Economics at Aarhus University*

"American critics of socialism frequently hear people say 'well, socialism works in Denmark!' *Danish Capitalism in the 20th Century: A Business History of an Innovistic Mixed Economy* is an important corrective to a simplistic narrative. By adopting a business history approach, Stefan K. Slok-Madsen explains the real source of Danish economic success: economic growth driven by innovism, not redistribution. If you're looking for a brief but comprehensive introduction to Danish economic history, this is the book to read."

—Art Carden *is a professor of economics at Samford University's Brock School of Business*

Contents

List of Figures

CHAPTER 1

Defining the Twentieth Century and Danish Capitalism

Good scientific inquiry revolves around the questions asked, more so than the answers given.[1] To ask good questions, clearly defined constructs are needed.[2] Therefore, I will use this chapter to clarify some important methodological considerations and define what is meant with the fundamental constructs utilized throughout this book, particularly the period in question, the version of capitalism under scrutiny, and how Denmark form a practical national example of a mixed economy.

[1] Gerald P. O'Driscoll, Mario J. Rizzo, & Roger W. Garrison, *The Economics of Time and Ignorance: With a New Introduction* (London: Routledge, 2002).

[2] David A. Whetten, "What Constitutes a Theoretical Contribution?", *Academy of Management Review*, 14:4 (1989), pp. 490–495; Christian Busse, Andrew P. Kach, & Stephan M. Wagner, "Boundary Conditions: What They Are, How to Explore Them, Why We Need Them, and When to Consider Them", *Organizational Research Methods*, 20:4 (2007), pp. 574–609.

© The Author(s), under exclusive license to Springer Nature Switzerland AG 2022

S. K. Sløk-Madsen, *Danish Capitalism in the 20th Century*, Palgrave Studies in Economic History,
https://doi.org/10.1007/978-3-031-04267-6_1

Individualist Methodology as a Historical Method

This book relies heavily on individualist methodology as the core causal relation of social change. This is not done without careful consideration of what this approach means for the validity, reliability, and boundary conditions of the analysis presented and exhumed.

Individualist methodology is often used in economics.[3] It holds that ultimately only the individual acts. While groups of individuals, like firms, definitely exist and can appear to act in unison, this is only appearance or a result of an agreement among choosing individuals. No collective, be it a firm, class, race, or whatever, acts. No abstraction, like nature, nation, or whatever, acts—only individuals acts.[4]

Furthermore, because individuals can reflect on their choices, we can judge them.[5] We can judge them morally or economically or in other ways. However, individualist methodology will only allow us to judge consequences, as actors' true intentions are not accessible to us but ultimately hidden in their consciousness.[6] However, we can judge the consequences, not because we hold that individual decision-makers have perfect foresight. Individuals are likely very limited in their capacity to understand the long-term and interrelated effects of their choices.[7] We can judge them because reflective individuals can choose to reflect on outcomes and alter future actions accordingly. As the saying goes, the highest level of stupidity is to keep doing the same thing and expect different results.

[3] James M. Buchanan & Gordon Tullock, *The Calculus of Consent: Logical Foundations of Constitutional Democracy* (Indianapolis: Liberty Fund, 1999).

[4] Ludwig Von Mises, *The Ultimate Foundation of Economic Science: An Essay on Method* (Indianapolis: Liberty Fund, 2006).

[5] Adam Smith, *The Theory of Moral Sentiments* (Indianapolis: Liberty Classics, 1976).

[6] On a practical note, this means that we can report what historical actors claim is their motivation, but only as a claim. We can also guess at motivation or intentions, but our conclusion must rest on observable consequences.

[7] Nicolai J. Foss & Libby Weber, "Moving Opportunism to the Back Seat: Bounded Rationality, Costly Conflict, and Hierarchical Forms", *Academy of Management Review*, 41:1 (2016), pp. 61–79; Richard N. Langlois, "Bounded Rationality and Behavioralism: A Clarification and Critique", *Journal of Institutional and Theoretical Economics*, 146 (1990), pp. 691–695.

As individuals are the ultimate lowest level of any social analysis according to individualist methodology, we are faced with several problems when investigating history. At a casual glance, the economist method of individual methodology appears similar to the great man theory of history. According to this theory, or strawman, history is only moved by the actions of a small group of unique individuals, most of whom we can name, like Napoleon, Stalin, or King Henry III. That would not be the right understanding of individualist methodology, however. While holding the acts of the individual at the micro level of analysis, the phenomenon in question is centered on the interplay and relation between actions of individuals, what economist calls a market. As such, a business history of Danish Capitalism in the twentieth century is for an individualist methodologist a story of market relations among agents in the institutional arrangement of Denmark in the twentieth century.

Telling a Grand National Narrative as an Individualist Methodologist

History can be approached in many different ways. Two main differences are between the sub-history and the grand historical narrative.[8] Sub-history views historical change through the lens of, or only concerning, a sub-section of the historical actors, like black history, women's history, and even some firm-centric or industry-centric types of business history. When it is fairly attempted, ***grand*** history is the attempt to tell history for all relevant actors, like a ***national*** history or some ***global industry*** history. As an individualist methodologist, telling a grand historical narrative describes market relations and their associated institutional arrangements over a period of time. However, institutions are not God-given, but a result of past individual actions and, as history unfolds, subject to alteration from the many choices of market actors living under them. Therefore, a significant part of this book will focus on the role of changing institutions and path dependency.[9]

[8] Jill Lepore, *These Truths: A History of the United States* (New York: W.W. Norton & Company, 2018).

[9] Susanna Fellman, Martin Jes Iversen, Hans Sjögren, & Lars Thue, *Creating Nordic Capitalism: The Business History of a Competitive Periphery* (New York: Palgrave Macmillan, 2008).

Boundary Conditions and Social Change

As explained above, for an individualist methodologist all social change originates in choices among market participants who, given mental and physical resource constraints, are morally free to choose how to best seek their utility satisfaction.[10] They are often wrong, but their modus operandi is still to exchange what they believe is a better situation for what they believe is a worse one. Disregarding individual preferences, social change results from individuals' pursuit of utility, be that social change intended or not. This approach also forms the primary boundary condition of the present work. If there should be a social element that is inter-human, genetic, theological, or in another way preordained, the individualist methodology will miss it altogether. This boundary condition is also a strength. In our investigation of historical development, we can ignore the actors' precise motivation and instead look at what happened and what it resulted in.

When Was the Twentieth Century in Denmark?

When I set out to work on this book, a fellow economist asked me what I foresaw as a big challenge. After pondering a bit, I replied: defining the twentieth century. He looked at me like I was silly and replied, that surely that was measured in dates. That is undoubtedly one way to limit and define the twentieth century taking as a point of reference that everything that happened from January 1, 1901 to December 31, 2000, is to be considered part of the twentieth century. There is also little doubt that time measurements like dates and hours do matter for human business organizing and outcomes.[11] This is also how a court might need to view the twentieth century if there is ever a court-case to preside over events in the twentieth century legally.

However, it is less fruitful for the current undertaking—explaining the interplay of society and business in shaping later economic outcomes. The reason is that the institutional arrangement and individuals' preferences

[10] While neoclassical economics often focus on utility maximization, a both more modern and classic interpretation of economic theory will hold the individuals seek satisfaction. For an introduction to the debate, see John Conlisk, "Why Bounded Rationality?", *Journal of Economic Literature*, 34:2 (1996), pp. 669–700.

[11] Lars Boerner, Jared Rubin, & Battista Severgnini, "A Time to Print, a Time to Reform", *European Economic Review*, 138 (2021), p. 103826.

do not form magically on a specific date. They are, much like a market equilibrium, in flux,[12] and actions before the event have consequences after. Much like the twentieth century as a social phenomenon does not just end at a specific time either.

If we instead try to see the period as not set by dates but by other aspects of the social experience, like ideas, events, institutions, etc., it is not impossible to imagine that a century as a historical period could both extend beyond the calendar dates, like the Hundred Years War (1337–1453), the Chinese Century of Humiliation (1839–1949), or even shrink to deal with a period less than the dates, like when referring to "21st-century skills"; such skills might change over the next 80 years after all. At least many of the most valuable skills in 1920 Denmark are far from today's. Therefore, the first challenge for this research is to define the twentieth century in Denmark.

As luck (or history) would have it, it is less complicated than what might be feared. There are dates close to the beginning and to the end that can be used—both are parliamentary system changes:

- 24 July 1901: This date is when governments were no longer appointed by the monarch but would be based on a parliamentary majority. While this practice of parliamentarism would not be part of the constitution (Grundloven) till 1953, it formed precedence from this date that the ruling government could not have a majority against it. While events leading up to the system change will be dealt with in Chapter 2, it is worth noticing that the change occurred after the conservative party Højre[13]—popular among big industry and nobility—lost to Venstre,[14] popular among small agriculture and the lesser bourgeois in towns. Hence the twentieth century starts with

[12] Ludwig M. Lachmann, *The Market as an Economic Process* (New York: Basil Blackwell, 1986).

[13] Højre literally translates into Right. The party as such no longer exist, but remnants of it is today present in the Conservative Peoples Party.

[14] Venstre literally translate into Left. The party still exists today but belongs on the right of the parliamentary spectrum. An issue of constant confusion to school children in social studies class and foreigners alike. The party is founded on classical liberal ideas but viewed largely through and adopted to the interest of agriculture, as will become clear in the book. To add further confusion, a spin-off from the Venstre party still existing today and is called "Radikale Venstre", literally translated to Radical Left. That party was for the majority of the twentieth century a center party.

one vision for Danish capitalism, claiming a major political victory over another vision for Danish capitalism.

- 27 November 2001: On this date, Anders Fogh Rasmussen (b. 1953) of Venstre takes over as Prime Minister of Denmark after the Social Democrat Poul Nyrup Rasmussen (b. 1943). While Chapter 7 will deal explicitly with the twenty-first century, the change of ruling coalition signified major shifts in Danish policy (and, by extension, capitalism). While economic reforms of the welfare state continued, most political attention turned away from economic matters toward issues relating to "Danish values",[15] at the same time as business organizations turned increasingly global.

These two milestones delineate the twentieth century in this book, and while not fitting the calendar century dates entirely, the timespan is pretty close. It is further possible to divide the century even further if one wishes to gain a quick overview of the century, and the book suggests this sectioning:

- 1901–1920: Parliamentary settlement

  As will be explained in Chapter 2, the widespread consensus at the beginning of the twentieth century was that Denmark's future was as a small nation in Europe that could be trusted and was open to trade. However, the question of national defense and the dukedoms in Schleswig Holstein remained a debated issue, and tension between parliament and king was not wholly settled, resulting in the parliamentary Easter Crisis of 1920 where King Christian X (1870–1947, monarch from 1912) dismissed the government. Faced with a potential revolution and the overthrow of the monarchy, the king backed down, and a new election was held. This was the last time the monarch interfered with politics without parliamentary backing.[16]

[15] Esben Schjørring & Michael Jannerup, *Værdikæmperne: Slaget om danskernes sjæl. VK-regeringerne 2001–2011* (Copenhagen: Gyldendal, 2018).

[16] According to the Danish Constitution the ruling monarch has to sign a law for it to become valid. This is one of the few checks and balances against majority rule in the Danish constitution. While in theory the monarch can refuse to sign a law, issues relating to this veto power is rare since 1920. However, Frederik IX who succeeded Christian X, and who was heavily tattooed refused to sign a law to ban tattoos, saying he would

- 1920–1940: Reunification, prosperity, and depression

  The period starts with the reunification with Sorthern Jutland, giving the Kingdom of Denmark the shape it currently has. While being an economically backward nation from 1600 compared to other European nations,[17] the many reforms had opened up the economy, and from 1870, the economy was booming.[18] While the global depression was most definitely felt in Denmark, the relative height of Danish prosperity was in the early 1930s, as shown in Fig. 1.1.[19] This period of prosperity, particularly the long period of sustained growth that preceded it, laid the economic foundations that would later make the welfare state an economic possibility. It is important to note that this period marked the end of the economic catch up effect for Danish economy; growing from poverty in 1600—particularly compared per capita to countries like the United Kingdom and the Netherlands—to the top of European countries for, more or less, the remainder of the century.[20]

- 1940–1945: German occupation

  Danish foreign policy had been almost exclusively focused on Germany for almost 150 years. The culmination was a German occupation in April 1940 that only met with nominal resistance. Despite the 150-year-old concern for why Denmark would be attacked by the neighbor to the South, the harsh truth was that Denmark was occupied on the way to secure the strategically more important Norway. Technology had made the world more global. While Danish policymakers still saw Denmark as a small European nation, it was now clear that Denmark was an

not sign anything that made him a criminal. A compromise was found where head (incl. neck), hand and feet tattooing was outlawed and the law signed in 1966.

[17] Per Boje, *Vejen til velstand - marked, stat og utopi: Om dansk kapitalismes mange former gennem 300 år. Tiden 1730–1850* (Odense: Syddansk Universitetsforlag, 2014).

[18] Per Boje, *Vejen til velstand - marked, stat og utopi: Hvorfor blev Danmark rigt–og ikke rigere? Tiden 1850–1930* (Odense: Syddansk Universitetsforlag, 2020).

[19] Olle Krantz, "Economic Growth and Economic Policy in Sweden in the Twentieth Century: A Comparative Perspective", *The Ratio Institute*, no. 32 (2004); Martin Ågerup, *Velfærd i det 21. århundrede* (Copenhagen: People's Press, 2017).

[20] World in Data and Madison Project.

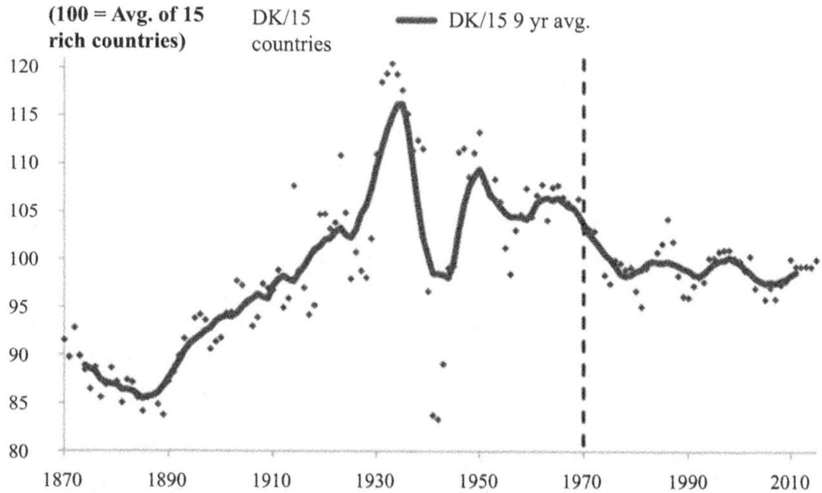

Fig. 1.1 Comparison of Danish wealth per capita to a peer group 1870–2015 (*Notes* For 1970–2015 is purchase power correlated GDP per capita in current prices from OECD. Prior to this, the graph is calculated based on the growth rates in fixed prices per capita from the Madison Project. The 15 countries are Australia, Austria, Belgium, Canada, Finland, France, Germany, Italy, Japan, Netherlands, Norway, Spain, Sweden, Switzerland, United Kingdom and USA. *Source* OECD Stat, Madison Project. From Ågerup, M., 2017. *Velfærd i det 21. århundrede*. Art People)

even smaller—relatively speaking—global nation. Danish business faced new challenges during the occupation. Firstly, unlike the politicians, business people were further ahead in reorienting themselves to an increasingly globalized world with shipping companies operating globally and many manufactures and procuderes of agricultural products having large exports to England, which were now lost. Secondly, whether and to what degree trading with the occupying force was acceptable was and remains a contested issue

- 1945–1953: Reorientation

The German occupation ended in May 1945. The following period saw economic hardship and a legal battle to settle blame for appeasement policies and actions during the occupation. Simultaneously, the global world was settling into a cold war stalemate, and a frantic race to reorient Denmark from the no longer important Germany to the Anglo-Saxon world began. Simultaneously, debates around the future of Danish society were booming and resulted in a constitutional reform in 1953.

- 1953–1976: Birth of the welfare state

  The actual birth of the welfare state in its universal model is hard to pinpoint and had some antecedents from 1890s. However, one major anchor point for the modern welfare state is the Bistandsloven (the aid law) of 1976, which both centralized and expanded the social benefits without requiring much in return of the recipients. Most subsequent governments have attempted to reign in and reshape the nature of welfare services. As the welfare state is a lasting institutional and economic legacy, Chapter 3 is primarily focused on the creation of it.

- 1976–1982: The death of utopia

  The welfare state quickly ran into difficulties. While the left suggested a new policy of "Economic Democracy" (in Danish: Økonomisk Demokrati), a scheme where employees would gradually take over firms, there was no escaping the dismal national economy. Denmark was among the worst-hit countries of the European Communities (the forerunner to EU) of the dreaded Keynesian decease: stagflation. The minister of Finance and budget, Knud Heinesen (b. 1932) went so far as to state on national television in 1979 that we were looking into the (economic) abyss. The period ended with a conservative-led coalition, not unlike those seen in other Western countries around the same time, taking over from a Social Democratic government who voluntarily admitted ideological defeat and gave up power without asking for a new election.

- 1982–2001: Reformation of the welfare state and new challenges

  Conservative and later Social Democratic-led governments started reform programs to fix the welfare state's broken business model, but still keeping within the universal welfare state ambition. The Cold War ended with the defeat of communism, and the nation was suddenly without a great enemy for the first time in its 1000-year history (German to Swedes to German to Russian).

Such was the Danish twentieth century at a glance, and in the coming chapters, some of these issues will be dealt with in more detail, while others in the interest of space will be left out. However, it is the aim to focus mainly on explaining firstly the lasting phenomenon (evt. phenomena, hvis der er flere), like the welfare state, and secondly the outcome, such as the commercial successes of the twenty-first century.

What Is Danish Capitalism?

There are many versions of capitalism. Most of the world today is governed by some version of capitalism. With an exact methodological disposition and a definition of the twentieth century, the next construct that needs to be scrutinized is the construct of *Danish Capitalism* as a version of capitalism.[21] Humans trade with each other because they are different and the issue of how to live together is why they form governments.[22] As such, markets as a way to organize outselves has been a naturally occurring phenomenon since the Stone Age some 13,000 years ago in the territorial area we now call Denmark.[23] Hence markets form primarily because they are efficient, but how efficient is institutionally contingent.

Unlike ideologies associated with either pro-markets (like classical liberalism) or anti-markets (like socialism) sentiments, there is no clear capitalist ideology. To some, true capitalism is a society exclusively based on property rights, freedom of contract, consent, and the rule of law. To others, the mere existence of barter or money makes a society capitalist. Others again see capitalism as a society based on the accumulation of capital assets via investments. The empirically observed institutional arrangement described as capitalist also varies significantly from

[21] Fellman et al., *Creating Nordic Capitalism: The Business History of a Competitive Periphery*.

[22] Buchanan & Tullock, 1999.

[23] Felix Riede, "Da himlen faldt ned", *Skalk*, no. 3 (2018), pp. 3–8.

completely anarchistic temporary situations to state-controlled economies like China.[24] Even Soviet Russia had to reintroduce some monetary exchange quickly after the revolution and relied heavily on the prices of the free market around them to coordinate and survive.[25] Today many nominal capitalist countries can be rightly accused of being so far under the sway of lobbying special interest groups from multinational corporations to unions that they are likely closer to crony capitalism than any (neo)liberal utopia (or dystopia depending on your political orientation). When trying to figure out what capitalism is in a Danish context, I will construct ***Danish Capitalism*** based on historical developments and observable Danish values, norms, traditions, and institutions.[26] My approach is similar to what has been called "Co-operative Liberalism", but certain details and weights differ.[27] It is hence not an ideology I promote, or one that can be attributed to any one political party. Instead, it is a thought system, as it has emerged with certain governing features all based from a strong state foundation. It is not a description of neither a dark nor a golden age—there is some argument as to whether there was a capitalist golden age in Denmark with some placing it from 1870 to 1920[28] while others place it in a post-World War II era.[29] I will argue that four of the features of Danish Capitalism are to be considered historically uncontested (academically, not politically), and five are emergent or historically still contestable. Figure 1.2 provides an overview.

[24] As examples see Edward Stringham, *Private Governance: Creating Order in Economic and Social Life* (Oxford: Oxford University Press, 2015); Peter T. Leeson, *WTF?!: An Economic Tour of the Weird* (Stanford: Stanford University Press, 2017); Peter T. Leeson, "Efficient Anarchy", *Public Choice*, 130:1–2 (2007), pp. 41–53.

[25] Peter J. Boettke, *Living Economics: Yesterday, Today, and Tomorrow* (Oakland: Independent Institute, 2012).

[26] Peter Skyum-Nielsen, *Arveguldet - Danskernes Værdier* (Odense: Syddansk Universitetsforlag, 2009).

[27] "Danish capitalism is an odd combination of British-influenced liberalism, German-inspired organization methods and Nordic egalitarian co-operatism", p. 263 in Fellman et al., *Creating Nordic Capitalism: The Business History of a Competitive Periphery*.

[28] Per Boje, 2020; Also features a narrative often subscribed to by Danish classical liberals.

[29] Balder Asmussen, "Danmark i kapitalismens guldalder: forholdet mellem den økonomiske politik og den samfundsøkonomiske udvikling i Danmark i 1950'erne", *Historisk Tidsskrift*, 104:2 (2004), pp. 430–449.

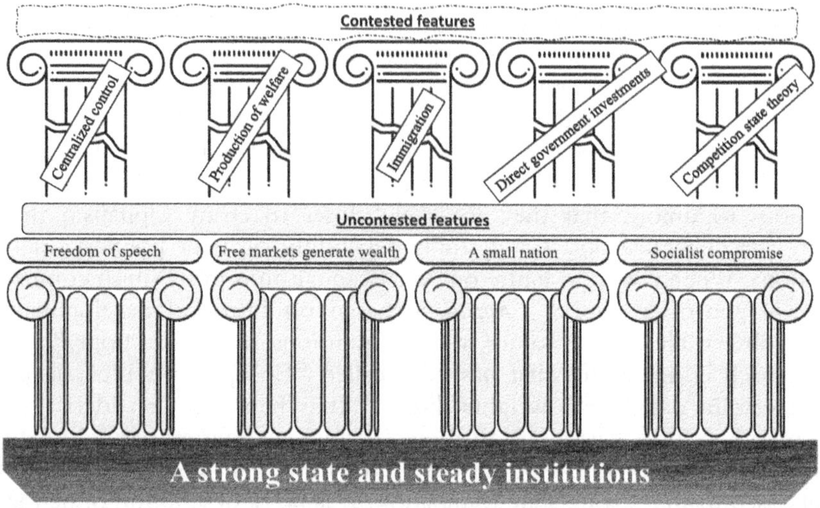

Fig. 1.2 The pillars of Danish capitalism

- The founding feature: A strong state and steady institutions
- After the loss of the Second Northern war (1655–1660) and provoked by the nobility tax refusals, King Frederik III (1609–1670, regent from 1648) in a coup instituted one of the most radical forms of absolutism in Europe. While most definitely a step toward totalitarianism, it also led to a professionalization of the bureaucracy and the legal system while opening up advancement based on merits rather than birth. This schism between a potentially all-ruling state and modern reform is essential to appreciate as it both at the time, and today, tends to give Danes a more pro-state attitude; even among classical liberals than what is found in other countries. From approximately 1800, gaining much speed from the 1864 defeat in the Second Schleswig War and culminating in the Easter Crisis (1920), the Danish state was further modernized and cemented into a strong state with low corruption and steady, trustworthy core institutions (while the government itself has been more volatile). It is

important to note that the foundation in the model is not related to the size of the state. The bloated and increasingly independently inefficient welfare state of the twenty-first century is far removed from the small state apparatus of both 1660 and 1901.

- Uncontested feature 1: Freedom of speech

  While the degree of totalitarianism varied from the hard religious pietism of Christian VI (1699–1746, monarch from 1730) to the liberal reform of Christian VII (1749–1808, monarch from 1766) and his privy counselor Johan Friedrich Struensee (1732–1772), there was no doubt as to who ruled, hence the matter of freedom of speech was therefore highly contested. Around 1770 to 1864, people like Peter Andreas Heiberg (1758–1841), Jens Baggesen (1764–1826), Karen Margrethe "Kamma" Rahbek (1775–1829), J. J. Dampe (1790–1867), and several others[30] started to debate the enlightenment ideas, and while it would take to 1848 to abolish absolutism, some clear insights can be deducted. Over the period, coupled with minor setbacks, it became clear that freedom of speech was both a fundamental good and an ingredient needed for innovation. On the more curious note, this resulted in Denmark being the first nation to legalize pornography on May 30, 1969, 6 years before Germany, whose Wiemar Republic years was likely the most sexually liberated pre-1968 and who had a long well-established nudist culture.[31] For a while, the position as early mover on legalized pornography made Denmark the international hotspot for commercial production and distribution of pornographic material.[32] Closer to the business side of things, the adherence to freedom of speech might also explain the flatter hierarchical structures

[30] Johan Bang, Martin Salmonsen, & Christian Borberg, *Frihedens sag er en borgerlig sag: Kampen om de borgerlige rettigheder 1770–1807: En antologi* (Varde: Dansklærerforeningen/Skov. 1984).

[31] Mel Gordon, *Voluptuous Panic: The Erotic World of Weimar Berlin (Expanded Edition)* (Los Angeles: Feral House, 2008); Richard Loxton, *Why Germany's Nudist Culture Remains Refreshing* (Bonn: Deutsche Welle, 2019).

[32] Bente Hansen, *Dengang i 60'erne: billeder fra dengang, tekster fra i dag* (Copenhagen: Information, 1978); Morten Thing, *Pornografiens Historie i Danmark* (Copenhagen: Lindhardt og Ringhof, 2018).

found in many Danish companies. It is also potentially likely that the lack of a class of powerful high nobility made freedom of speech a truly bottom-up idea.

- Uncontested feature 2: Free markets based on property rights generate wealth

The Denmark of absolutism was restrictive to business and competition. Policies like vornedskab[33] and Stavnsbåndet[34] limiting citizens' movement, large custom duties existed, especially on what people at the time considered luxury goods; and industry and trade privileges granted to specific cities and individuals also limited entrepreneurship and competition. The removal of these types of regulatory constraints and the following speedy and general improvement in welfare is pivotal to understand, as the public at large experienced the power of markets.[35] This was seen many years later when the working classes refused rented dwelling in council estates build on Social Democratic principles in the 1960s and opted for small independent and privately owned housing (parcelhuse in Danish)—today well over 50% of Danes live in privately owned homes (ejerbolig). Danish Capitalism is a constant trade-off between the power of the free market and other concerns,[36] be they troops to fight Sweden or union monopolizing workforces

[33] These policies were forms of serfdom that stipulated peasants must stay in their birth county and work there. Vornedskab was introduced after the Black Death in the fourteenth century to ensure peasants would not go where they were offered the best terms by the often desperate nobility at the time. It was abolished in 1702, but Stavnsbåndet in 1733 reintroduced similar serfdom policy after many peasants had left their former homes behind to seek better fortunes elsewhere, mainly in towns. As an interesting sidenote, outside the Copenhagen Central Station is a large monument called the Liberty Memorial (Frihedsstøtten) erected in 1788 when Stavnsbåndet was abolished, but conscription introduced. It seems Danish liberty is at the mercy of the state. See Tine Damsholt, *Fædrelandskærlighed og borgerdyd: patriotisk diskurs og militære reformer i Danmark i sidste del af 1700-tallet*, Vol. 6. (Copenhagen: Museum Tusculanum, 2000).

[34] Ibid.

[35] Karsten Ronit, "Handelens vej er altid kulturens vej, Det Danske Handelskammer 1742–1992", *Historie*, no. 19, (Aarhus: Jysk selskab for historie, 1991), p. 774.

[36] Niels Thomsen, "Industri, stat og samfund, 1870–1939", in Hans Chr. Johansen et al., *Dansk industri efter 1870*, Vol. 3 (Odense: Odense Universitetsforlag, 1988).

via laws—a common labor market conflict today.[37] Also, for Danish Capitalism the firm is a "Fundamental institution",[38] that allows planning over usage of property rights for production and is judged by profit.[39] The visible hand of management hand shaking the invisible hand of the market.[40]

- Uncontested feature 3: A small nation

  A more contested issue historically, but not today, was the question of the ideal size of Denmark. The kingdom - or nationstate in its entirety is relatively small, but simultaneously, and to this day, the Danish monarch rules over a Commonwealth (Rigsfællesskabet). For an extended period of time, a debate arose as to whether the interests of the Danes were best served with as large a landmass under the rule as possible—including the problems that come along with that e.g. national minorities, or as a small country. While the debate initially supported the former, the defeat against Prussia in 1864 cemented Denmark as a smaller nation. From that period, the national narrative changed and centered on being small and trustworthy; with low levels of corruption, fair courts and with steady institutions and strong work ethics, while simultanously being very open to trade. Monetary policy is a good representation of this; while maintaining a national currency, the exchange rate has been tied to the German D-mark and Euro since 1982. It is, however, further necessary to note that, besides oil and gas, the nation holds very little in terms of national resources and are hence further required to trade, but it is at the same time traditionally

[37] In Chapter 6, we will return to the flexicurity model of the Danish labor market. It is too comprehensive to touch on here, but for the sake of analysis, it fits under this feature in the model.

[38] Fellmann et al., *Creating Nordic Capitalism: The Business History of a Competitive Periphery*.

[39] Alfred D. Chandler, *The Visible Hand: The Managerial Revolution in American Business* (Cambridge, MA: Harvard University Press, 1993); Frederic Sautet, *An Entrepreneurial Theory of the Firm* (London: Routledge, 2000).

[40] The visible hand of the market is an allegory attributed to Adam Smith. The visible hand of management to Alfred Chandler and Ronald Coase, and the handshake to Walter A. Friedman, *Birth of a Salesman: The Transformation of Selling in America* (Cambridge, MA: Harvard University Press, 2004).

large enough to have national providers of key infrastructure like trains in the past and telcos in more modern times; whether technological developments are again taking over in this area is a slighlty more contested area today such as in regards to e.g. 5G networks or the impact on democracy from social media.

- Uncontested feature 4: Socialist compromise

  One of the first welfare states was developed by the conservative Otto von Bismarck (1815–1898) in an attempt to stop the rise of socialism; by tying people's economic interests to the state with a shared pension pool.[41] Similarly understanding Danish Capitalism cannot be done without understanding the impact of Danish Social Democratism. From a rocky start, Denmark's Social Democratic movement grew because it broke with several Marxist beliefs. Firstly, they accepted a liberal reform approach and outwardly rejected revolution as a beneficial path for working-class interests. Secondly, they accepted markets as fundamentally essential and often superior to state planning.[42] The state's role was to create a somewhat level playing field where the spoils of market activity could be redistributed to non-market participants. This compromise with liberalism became more popular than the pure Marxist version of socialism. This no less became important in that the Social Democrats took over control of the trade unions and actively fought communist tendencies within the worker's rights movements—helped by growing prosperity and growth from capitalism. As the old Danish Social Democratic party slogan goes: "Do your duty—demand your right" (gør din plight, kræv din

[41] Christopher Pierson & Francis G. Castles (eds.), *The Welfare State Reader* (Cambridge: Polity Press, 2006); Tom G. Palmer (ed.), *After the Welfare State: Politicians Stole Your Future... You Can Get It Back* (Ottawa: Jameson Books, 2012). An important note is that one of the clear policy successes of the late twentieth century Danish Capitalism was the pension reforms under Prime Minister Poul Schlüter (1929–2021). However, these are somewhat independent and individualistic and very much a market-driven reform program.

[42] This is not to say that many Social Democratic devotees are not skeptical of markets and market participants. They often are.

ret)—Socialist aspirations should be accomplished by trade and parliamentary compromise.

I will argue that these four features plus the strong state form the basis of Danish Capitalism and is relatively uncontested. There are further five potential features that are more contested issues from an academic or historical viewpoint.

- Contested feature 1: Centralized control

    The population of Denmark is roughly that of the greater metropolitan area of Philadelphia in the United States and the area and economic output comparable to that of Lower Saxony in Germany. Nevertheless, Danes often believe there to be longer from Hirtshals to Copenhagen than from Hirtshals to Cape Verde. Part of this has to do with the fact that the Danish institutional arrangement and civil law legal system is at least in part modeled on a French ideal of centralization. Indeed, Copenhagen is the center for much economic growth and political activity in Denmark.[43] Throughout the twentieth and continued into the twenty-first century, we saw this centralization bias expressed in reforms of municipal government and the tax authority, among other areas. There are, however, clear voices that throughout the time period, have been calling for more local autonomy, the most recent development being the forced and somewhat random relocation of certain governmental authorities and offices to all corners of the kingdom. All in all, the question of centralized or decentralized control of a pretty small territorial area should be considered contested.

- Contested feature 2: Production of welfare supply

    While there today seems to be, to a large extent, somewhat of a consensus on—significant redistribution of income, wealth, and property via taxes, it does not need to be so for the production of welfare services. Especially, private firms are so much more efficient in other aspects of Danish life. While today, the state

[43] At the time of writing, Greater Copenhagen generated roughly 40% of Danish GDP.

owns and controls near monopolies within health care, nurseries, school, elder- and handicap care, it is a contested issue. Particularly as public organizations are less efficient, slower to innovate, and that technology might open up for better solutions, which are harder to experiment with for the public sector. Hence, the degree of outsourcing of production of welfare is more debatable than redistribution. The state has privatized the telecommunication industry to great consumer utility, while maintaining a railway company to large consumer dis-utility. Areas such as postal services, airfare and energy are state-owned to various degrees, but exposed to competition and consumer choice. There are also clear ideological fault lines in whether profit-seeking is a feature or a bug of private welfare production, where especially the left-wing and its proponents have been working hard to dismantle the markets for private welfare production.

- Contested feature 3: Immigration

While significant numbers of Danes did migrate to The New World, the immigration tradition is less pronounced in Denmark than in other nations; the reasons are manifold.[44] Partly, immigration was legally more challenging for Danes at times, and at other times, opportunities at home were interesting enough, mainly during the second industrial revolution, to keep people home. We do observe that many important businesspeople spent time in foreign countries, such as C. F. Tietgen (1829–1901), just like today. A famous example is Carlsberg, which was founded by people who had spent time in other nations and learned new ideas they imported. Today as well, the large global Danish companies rely strongly on a global workforce, often attracted by a temporarily lower tax for foreign specialists, from chemists to footballers. The very easy access to education for young Danes impact educational choices, and likely also increases the need for non-skilled foreign labor, as people with college degrees rarely want to pick strawbarries, but also might not have the skills requested at

[44] In fact, the US government officially complained several times that Denmark exported criminal elements to the new world.

the college end of labor demand (for all its merits a person with a masters degree within the humanities is rarely skilled in designing concrete bridges). On the society level, the picture is muddier. For most of the twentieth century, non-European foreigners were a rare sight in Denmark. However, a mix of a short-term need for migrant workers and open borders, asylum seekers and very lenient immigration laws passed in the 1980s means that 8.8% of the population having a non-Western background today. A larger share of these individuals compared, to other groups, is a net cost to the welfare state, and the ghettoization and failed immigration schemes have been the principal political topic in the twenty-first century. On the other hand, the open market for labor within the EU has benefited Danish citizens tremendously. Thus the role and importance of immigration and foreign labor is a contested feature of Danish Capitalism.

- Contested feature 4: Direct government investments

From the earliest days of Danish state formation, the state has been an active economic player, including within the area of direct business ventures. During the twentieth century, the role of the state in industry investments has been debated. The involvement has not always been in direct investment, but often in tax breaks and favorable legislation to specific business interests. The most debated modern example is likely the wind turbine industry. Direct investments in entrepreneurs have been significant. Whether these policy initiatives have had a good return on investment compared to the opportunity cost and who benefited and on behalf of who is highly debatable and an interesting case for future historical studies.

When the dynamics and creative destruction of capitalism threatens companies and sometimes entire industries or regions, politicians can be tempted to fight the current of change to protect current jobs.[45] The Danish welfare state was largely politically possible in exchange for agricultural industry favors. The bail-out of Scandinavian Airlines provides examples of

[45] Joseph A. Schumpeter, *Capitalism, Socialism and Democracy* (New York: Harper Perennial, 2009).

political protection of selected firms and industries, but it also seems that when Danish policymakers have withstood the temptation to interfere, the market has provided better solutions. Two examples come to mind. The Jutland textile industry was booming while protected but withered under real international competition. However, the region in the period had lower than average wages and worse living conditions. Today, it is among the most prosperous areas in Denmark, including creating impressive global fashion conglomerates—like Bestseller. Another example is the large-scale closing of Danish ship construction industry toward the end of the twentieth century. From 5 shipyard closings grew 27 innovative companies—several now global market leaders—and among the 9400 employees tracked most found better paid labor elsewhere.[46]

- Contested feature 5: Competition state theory

In recent times, a new theory has developed and taken a large hold in the Danish understanding of ***Danish Capitalism***. The theory is called Competition State Theory, which was introduced in Denmark by political scientist Ove Kaj Pedersen and others.[47] The theory argues that the competition state has taken over from the welfare state. The argument goes that the focus has changed for policy, so the state is to create a framework that enables it and the nation's companies to outcompete other nations and their citizens—a modern version of mercantilism. It is further the citizens' role to optimize themselves, such as their educational choices, for this goal, and the state should incentivize them toward this. This "neo mercantilism" has impacted policy, education, and culture to an astonishing degree in the twenty-first century. This book will still consider the theory contested as much historical knowledge and economic theory contradicts its merits. Firstly, the theory explaining markets as created by the state is not supported by economics and history. Secondly, the market concept used is

[46] Thomas Roslyng Olesen, *Da værfterne lukkede: Transformationen af den danske værftsindustri 1975–2015* (Odense: Syddansk Universitetsforlag, 2016).

[47] Ove K. Pedersen, *Konkurrencestaten* (Copenhagen: Hans Reitzels Forlag, 2011).

one of the winner takes all, rather than the positive-sum game observed in most market transaction. Thirdly, the application of competition is not the one typically understood by economist as a coordinating and disciplinary force, but rather more like a war-like situation. Fourthly, the theory, to a large extent, assumes that policymakers (in both government and companies) hold knowledge about the future they cannot have.[48] Fifthly, the theory attributes positive features to the welfare state that are debatable. Finally, it has an overemphasis on the importance of political decision-making in social outcomes. However, the theory is right in that the reform agenda of the twentieth century has been focused on optimization of the welfare sector—but that is also not the same as dismantling it. However, the core reality of the welfare state remains and the fact that Denmark since 1996 has been in the top two highest tax rate in Europe (most years as number 1) and that the number of voters who primarily???? from state income (employment and benefits) is still growing and well over 60%, contradicts the theory in this author's opinion.[49] Competition State theory seem like a "welfare national romantic" idealization that appeals to special interest, but holds little explanatory power for why Danish Capitalism and firms (who largely employ non-Danes) are as we observe today.

Danish Capitalism as a Case for Innovism

When explaining the astonishingly and, so far unique, ability to generate prosperity, most scholars of capitalism highlight capital accumulation or institutional arrangement as the key explanatory factors. However, we have had periods in the past where capital was accumulated, and we have also had favorable institutions in certain areas and at certain times without seeing the same result. This prompted McCloskey to insist on highlighting innovative capacity as the actual interesting features of the

[48] Friedrich August von Hayek, "The Use of Knowledge in Society", *The American Economic Review*, 35:4 (1945), pp. 519–530.

[49] The international comparison is a more complex subject, where the tax status of welfare transfers, VAT, fiscal policy, capital, and other property tax plays a role, as well as tax authority effectiveness. Needless to say Denmark is in the top of the world here.

Great Enrichment of modern times that caused the production possibility frontier to grow by a factor of thirty.[50] She therefore renames capitalism, innovism. Rather than focusing on capital (of any kind) accumulations, which has diminishing returns, innovism focuses on the interaction of institutions on novel ideas, the freedom to try something new.

The explanation is extremely interesting in a Danish context. The early debates around freedom of speech and freedom of trade are both key innovism ingredients. The state's early focus on education in the nineteenth century reforms coupled with prosperity growth from markets providing leisure time to attend more school for more people likely increased the quality of ideas and paved the way for new ideas—especially from outside the country to spread. As necessity is often the mother of invention, the resource poor and militarily weak national situation from 1864 likely provided further imperative to innovation too.[51] Conversely, the modern welfare state of the second half of the twentieth century might be a negative interaction effect on idea generation and assimilation. This would however not disprove McCloskey's point—merely give more merit to the concept.

The Mixed Economy: Balancing of a Regulatory State and the Free Market

This chapter has outlined how to understand historical outcomes, how the book is investigating them, and the ideas that have guided developments (while simultaneously being developed themselves—what economics might call interaction effects). I will end this chapter by tying all this together to the overall research aim. Today Denmark is a mixed economy with several globally relevant companies. It is a small country with a large and strong state committed to a universal welfare state ideal dependent on a healthy free market to generate state-funding for said welfare.

In the model in Fig. 1.2, the state was taken very much for granted, but it is a crucial antecedent that the state is strong and fairly efficient. At the

[50] For an expansion of the argument, see Deirdre N. McCloskey, "Liberalism—Caused the Modern World", *CEPOS* (2021), https://CEPOS.dk/debat/liberalism-caused-the-modern-world/, Accessed Jan 21, 2022.

[51] Svend Aage Hansen, "Økonomisk vækst i Danmark. I. 1720–1914", *Institut for Økonomisk historie* (Copenhagen: Københavns Universitet, 1977).

same time, the government has been very tumultuous. Massive redistribution, for instance, requires an efficient tax system. Since 1968, Denmark has made use of a personal identification number (CPR number) that is so important for the welfare state that it is given instantaneously at birth (whereas naming can wait 6 months). Such a system, which is not without its challenges in modern times[52] is also efficient for companies who likewise make use of it to a great extent. In fact, it likely creates trust as everyone is personally identifiable by it and very limited in their agency if not using it. It is perhaps a perfect illustration of a mixed economy, the need of the state creates possibilities for companies too.

It is, however, a delicate balance, and the trade-offs are many and keep occurring. After explaining the development of Danish society and its antecedents, we will in Chapter 4 discuss competing explanations for Danish prosperity. Chapter 5 will then showcase important Danish businesses and industries before in Chapter 6 investigating some unique methods of Danish Capitalism. Chapter 7 will, as earlier alluded to, look at the first two decades of the twenty-first century before finally ending the book with concluding remarks.

[52] As everything from personal finances to medical history is tied to the number, data security is essential, yet the system was not designed for that and have seen massive leaks, in the other end of the scale, queer activists are angry that the system identifies binary genders.

CHAPTER 2

Antecedents to Danish Capitalism in the Twentieth Century

Roughly speaking,[1] the basic Danish narrative is often interpreted as a version of the fairy tale *The Ugly Duckling*, written by the world-famous Danish poet H. C. Andersen (1805–1875).[2] The ugly past grew up to be a beautiful modern future. As such the history of Denmark is described as a harmonized transition from a consensus-monarchy to a consensus democracy that laid the groundwork for a modern Danish, Social Democratic welfare state.[3]

I am fundamentally dismissive of this basic narrative. First and foremost because it is ideologically Social Democratic and marked by the nineteenth-century romantic notion of Denmark as a fairytale country. Just like fairytales, it is at best good entertainment, but as a historical narrative, it is insufficient of empirical evidence and often lacking a much-needed historical context. Fortunately, Danish historical research writing

[1] See Chapter 1.

[2] Sissel Bjerrum Fossat, Rasmus Glenthøj, & Lone Kølle Martinsen (eds.), *Konfliktzonen Danmark: Stridende fortællinger om dansk historie* (Copenhagen: Gads Forlag, 2018).

[3] Jeppe Nevers, *Det produktive samfund: seks kapitler af industrialiseringens idéhistorie* (Odense: Syddansk Universitetsforlag, 2013).

© The Author(s), under exclusive license to Springer Nature Switzerland AG 2022

S. K. Sløk-Madsen, *Danish Capitalism in the 20th Century*, Palgrave Studies in Economic History,
https://doi.org/10.1007/978-3-031-04267-6_2

has undergone a development over the past 10 years and has been seriously challenged, especially by economic and liberal historians.[4] I put myself in the same critical slipstream, which is why this chapter, as well as other historical passages in this book, is based on parts of the incipient counter-narrative about Danish growth and welfare in the nineteenth and twentieth centuries.

In this chapter, I will explain in particular that one of the main reasons for Denmark's development was to a greater extent due to a series of historical *trade-offs* between the state (both as a monarchy and later limited democracy) and its subjects, the later Danish citizens. Instead of reproducing the harmonized consensus history, I will present a counter-narrative focused on the Danish conditions, in the years after democratization in 1849, and the subsequent liberal reforms until the year 1901 with the introduction of parliamentarism.

The Ancient Danish Folk

The Danes as a tribe or a culture are ancient. We know humans have populated present-day Denmark for at least 14,000 years.[5] The oldest written account of the Danes is from the East Gothic Ravenna Court from the middle of the 500s.[6] Such longevity is impressive on its own. Hundreds—if not thousands—of tribes, nations, and civilizations have perished in this enormous span of time.

- Homo sapiens originated around 200,000 years ago, and hence have populated Denmark for 7% of that time.
- A concept of Danes has existed close to 1% of humanity's biological existence.

If we, a bit cheekily, were to talk about the Danes as a civilization, it has in other words outlasted more famous periods in world history such as

[4] Per Boje, *Danmark og multinationale virksomheder før 1950* (Odense: Odense Universitetsforlag, 2000); Fossat et al. (eds.), *Konfliktzonen Danmark*.

[5] Torsten Günther, Helena Malmström, Emma M. Svensson, Ayça Omrak, Frederico Sánchez-Quinto, Gülşah M. Kılınç, Maja Krzewińska, et al., "Population Genomics of Mesolithic Scandinavia: Investigating Early Postglacial Migration Routes and High-Latitude Adaptation", *PLoS Biology*, 16:1 (2018), p.e. 2003703.

[6] Kasper H. Andersen, "Danerne og Ravanna", *Skalk*, no. 1 (2018).

the Mesopotamians and The Roman Empire, and it still exists. According to the lindy effect, the longer something has existed, the more likely it is to survive.[7] This alone makes Danish society and its institutional arrangements an interesting phenomenon to study.

If we try to pinpoint Denmark as a nation, we can look to the Danish monarchy which is at least dating from around 970—but likely further back. This makes the Danish monarchy one of the oldest in the world. The first two kings, Gorm the Old and Harald Bluetooth,[8] set a national birth certificate in stone in the world heritage site Jelling. Relevant for this book, is the engraving on the back of Harald's stone—a motive also printed in the Danish passport. It likely depicts a lion or a horse and a serpent entangled in each other. Archaeologists call the symbol, the "battle motif" and long debates exist about what "battle" it refers to, between king and lords, Christianity and Norse beliefs, Denmark and Norway, etc.[9] I interpret the motif differently. I think it outlines an understanding of society as a trade-off and a political promise or even contract between the central authority and the people. Society is a dance—potentially both violent and fun—between a free civil society and a strong state. Which animal represents what is up to one's own interpretation or might actually change dependent on the situation. Or maybe the horse is the market, as the horse was in many ways the height of production technology at the times, and the snake the state—this would make sense, as one of the few enemies of the snake is the eagle—the symbol of the German Empire. Harald was communicating that he understood that without a rich free society, there was nothing to rule, and that the state should both protect and be paid by the riches of the market. A true trade-off as economists would understand it (Fig. 2.1).

On October 30, 1536, Denmark became officially became Lutheran. Part of that belief system is that people are to be baptized as babies, but should freely confirm their faith in a ritual as they come of proper age. In a way, the Danish nation too confirmed the Harald vision when adscription was replaced with national conscription in 1788. The occasion

[7] Nassim Nicholas Taleb, *Skin in the Game: Hidden Asymmetries in Daily Life* (New York: Random House, 2018).

[8] The communication technology of the same name is indeed named after King Harald. See https://www.eetimes.com/tech-history-how-bluetooth-got-its-name/?page_number=1#.

[9] Anna Vebæk Gelskov, "'Det store dyr' igennem tiden", *Skalk*, no. 3 (2021).

Fig. 2.1 The Jelling Stone depiction (*Note* The Jelling Stone right and the passport artwork [left]. *Source* Gelsko 2021)

was marked by another stone monument in 1792, the Liberty Memorial. On it reads (my translation): "*A just rule is one, which provide the citizen liberty, and which in turn can expect the citizen to be faithful to the nation, work for the benefit of their fellow citizen, aspire towards high work ethic, such a work ethic that will provide the country with riches and citizens willing to defend their nation*".

I argue in this book that also today, the essence of Denmark and Danish Capitalism is the dance, balance, or battle of competing social forces; a free-market civil society and a strong state. But before we can affirm this old national essence in current times and how it came to be shaped in the twentieth century, we will start by examining the preceding nineteenth century in broad strokes focusing on how the overall frame of Denmark in the twentieth century was formed.

Danish Downfall in the Nineteenth Century

At the beginning of the nineteenth century, Denmark was no longer the regional superpower, neither militarily nor economically, that had otherwise characterized the country in the previous 300 years. Denmark as a state was a dual monarchy consisting of a personal union with Norway, including a number of duchies in the Northern Germany—Schleswig, Holstein, and Lauenburg[10]—as well as the Danish colonial possessions in the Danish West Indies, the Gold Coast of Africa, and the tropical colonies at the Bay of Bengal, respectively; Tranquebar, Serampore, Gondalpara, Oddeway Torre, and the Nicobar Islands.

The reasons for Denmark's decline in the eighteenth century can generally be characterized by three things: (1) The economically exhaustive and destructive wars with neighboring Sweden.[11] (2) The European alliance-dynamics, which had effectively left Denmark isolated, both in terms of military measures as well as in bilateral agreements, in the strictly closed and mercantilist European economy,[12] and (3) Poor statesmanship, rooted in a number of inefficient absolutist Danish monarchs, poorly guided by a strongly conservative State Council.[13]

The French Revolution and the later takeover of France by Napoleon gave the Danish monarch Frederik VI (1768–1839, monarch from 1808, regent form 1784 due to his father's mental issues) the opportunity to regain the Danish prestige and grandeur of earlier times, even though the path to the Danish-Franco alliance was more or less entered involuntarily.

[10] The duchy of Lauenburg became a Danish possession after the Treaty of Kiel in 1814. Originally, Lauenburg were on French hands, who handed Lauenburg to Prussia after the Napoleonic Wars, who then again traded the province to Sweden, in return for the Swedish part of Pomerania. To ease the Danish loss of Norway, Sweden gave the province to the Danes.

[11] Rasmus Glenthøj & Morten Nordhagen Ottosen, "1814: Krig, Nederlag Frihed: Danmark-Norge Under Napoleonskrigene", *Historisk Tidsskrift*, 94:1 (2016), pp. 180–184.

[12] Knud J.V. Jespersen & Ole Feldbæk, *Revanche og neutralitet 1648–1814: Dansk Udenrigspolitiks historie*, Vol. 2 (København: Danmarks Nationalleksikon, 2002).

[13] Ole Feldbæk, "Den lange fred", In: Olaf Olsen (ed.), *Gyldendals og Politikens Danmarkshistorie*, Vol. 9 (Copenhagen: Gyldendal, 1991); Claus Bjørn, "Fra reaktion til grundlov", In: Olaf Olsen (ed.), *Gyldendals og Politikens Danmarkshistorie*, Vol. 10 (Copenhagen: Gyldendal, 1991).

As part of the French Revolutionary Wars, Denmark had entered into a neutrality alliance with Russia, Sweden, and Prussia in order to minimize the risk of getting involved in the Franco-British strife. In 1801, Britain demanded that Denmark left the neutrality alliance, as the British feared that Denmark would join the French side. The British further demanded that the Danes lend their fleet to Great Britain, an ultimatum Frederik VI chose to oppose.[14] The rejection of the British demand was the warning shot to Denmark's involvement in the later Napoleonic Wars.

While France had initial success in this series of major European wars in the first decades of the nineteenth century, the conclusion of the Napoleonic Wars was French defeat, and a by-product of it, an even further Danish humiliation on the European stage. As part of the peace negotiations in 1814, Denmark was to cede Norway to arch-rival Sweden after 434 years of Danish-Norwegian personal union.[15] In addition to the territorial concessions in the form of Norway, Denmark's involvement in the Napoleonic Wars had weighed heavily on the Danish state finances, which resulted in Denmark going bankrupt the same year, 1814.[16] Thus the beginning of the nineteenth century was thus the direct opposite of what Frederik VI had imagined for Denmark. Instead of having achieved the splendor and grandeur of the past, the country was now a decimated and penniless small state on the European fringe.[17]

The Collective State Model

In the years after the defeat of the war, with its territorial and economic consequences, Denmark was characterized by widespread stagnation. The stagnation did not only apply to the economic paradigm of Danish governance but also to the constitutional division and management of what in Danish historiography is referred to as *the collective state* (Danish: Helstaten). Helstaten is a term for the central state formation in Denmark, in the years after 1814 until the adoption of Danish constitution in 1849. Previously, the possessions of the Danish state had been described as

[14] Lars Lindeberg, *Englandskrigene 1801–1814* (Copenhagen: Lademann, 1974).

[15] Georg Nørregård, *Freden i Kiel 1814* (Copenhagen: Rosenkilde og Bagger, 1954).

[16] Knud Erik Svendsen, *Dansk pengehistorie*, Vol. 1 (Copenhagen: Danmarks Nationalbank, 1968).

[17] Jespersen & Feldbæk, *Revanche og neutralitet 1648–1814*.

a sort of empire, but with the departure of the kingdoms' Norwegian domain, the state structure was now more divided. In practice, Helstaten consisted of four elements: (1) The Kingdom: Denmark, Jutland north of the Kongeå, Zealand, Funen, and Bornholm. (2) The North-German duchies: Schleswig, Holstein, and Lauenburg. (3) The North Atlantic dependent territories: the Faroe Islands and Iceland. And (4) The Danish colonies: including Greenland, Danish possessions in the West Indies, India, and the African Gold Coast.

It is especially in the North-German duchies that the Danish state's new system becomes important. In addition to being the possessions of the state-structure Helstaten, the duchies were also part of the newly founded German Confederation.[18] In the aftermath of the Napoleonic Wars, the Estates Assembly movement (Danish: Stænderforsamlingerne) in the duchies began to demand increased autonomy and representation.[19]

The duchies, unlike the rest of the kingdom, were not connected to Denmark as a state domain, but instead bound directly to the king and the Danish monarchy. Throughout Danish history, the status of the duchies has given rise to a number of twists and turns for Danish kings' involvement in European affairs, most famous being Christian IV's (1577–1648) involvement in the Thirty Years' War. Here, the State Council opposed that Christian IV as Danish regent could participate in the war, instead he participated in the war as the Duke of Schleswig and Holstein, which the kings' State Council could not prevent, as it were not the Kingdom of Denmark's, but the king's personal domain.[20]

In order to maintain the unity of the kingdom, King Frederik VI chose to establish Estates Assemblies in 1831, not only in the duchies as purposed, but also for the rest of the kingdom. The Estate Assemblies were initially only of an advisory nature and consisted only of a few

[18] The duchies were held by the Danish monarch as a duke, but not integrated as a part of the Danish Kingdom.

[19] Carsten Porskrog Rasmussen, *Hertugdømmet* (Aarhus: Aarhus Universitetsforlag, 2019).

[20] Anders Olling & Hans Erik Havsteen, *Christian 4* (Copenhagen: Lindhardt og Ringhof, 2018).

major landowners, wealthy city landowners, city merchants, and large-scale farmers.[21] Through the 1830s, these advisory assemblies initiated the first public policy discussions in Denmark, the king, who had been reluctant in relinquishing parts of his absolute power, had to profess that the advisory Estate Assemblies were capable of producing the crucial political innovation which was necessary for the survival of the diminished state.[22]

By the beginning of the 1840s, the Estate Assemblies, in consultation with the State Council, had implemented increased municipal self-government for Copenhagen, the privileged market towns and rural municipalities, and had revised and liberalized the Danish customs.[23] By the mid-1840s, the joint actions of the Estate Assemblies and the State Council had effectively regained control of the state's finances, restarted Danish agriculture and production, and thereby lifted Denmark out of the economic nightmare that 20 years before was threating to tear the country apart.[24] The solution had been simple; the liberalization of trade and decentralization of the state, another chapter in the age old and still today ongoing Danish centralization debate.

The First Constitution

When Frederik VI died in 1839, Christian VIII (1786–1848) ascended to the throne as the Danish autocratic king. In contrast to Frederik VI, the new king was of a more liberal mind and had during his time in the State Council, shown sympathy for the Danish National Liberal movement, which wanted a greater degree of democratization and liberalization of trade, as well as the Estates' demands for increased autonomy. In Danish liberal circles, therefore, the new regent was viewed positively, and there was an expectation that he would work for a free constitution, which he had done during his short reign as King of Norway in the short period

[21] Steen Bo Frandsen, *Opdagelsen af Jylland: Den regionale dimension i danmarkshistorien 1814–64*. 1. ed. (Aarhus: Aarhus Universitetsforlag, 1996).

[22] Jens Engberg, *Den standhaftige tinsoldat: en biografi om Frederik 6* (Copenhagen: Politiken, 2009).

[23] Steen Busck, Henning Poulsen, & Helge Paludan (eds.), *Danmarks historie - i grundtræk* (Aarhus: Aarhus Universitetsforlag, 2011).

[24] Ibid.

from May 17 to October 10, 1814.[25] As king, Christian VIII disappointed the National Liberal movement in their desire for a Danish free constitution. Instead, the king tried to accommodate the democratic and liberal movements by modernizing and stabilizing the autocratic Helstat, therefore, he has historically been termed by historians as a 'Helstats-conservative'. For the German estate assemblies in the duchies, he also changed course when he took over the throne, instead of continuing the previous line of increased autonomy in the Danish-German possessions, he actively sought to Danishize the duchies and make them an active bulwark against the German states south of the border.[26] In early 1843 the king wrote in his diary (my translation):

> *The year begins with me with joyful courage in trusting in God's assistance. Among the Morning Hymns I listed one of Boye,*[27] *in which it is said that only the Kingdom is happy, in which peace reigns. It occurred to me that this is less than ever the case in my kingdom, where the party spirit, nurtured between Denmark and the duchies, breeds discord. I therefore prayed to God that he would give me wisdom and power to settle these strifes, which are nurtured by exaggerations on both sides, as the Schleswig-Holsteins would simply clarify Schleswig. The Danish Radicals, on the other hand, want to tear Schleswig completely out of Holstein. The King should stand over the parties and maintain the condition as it is: Schleswig as a separate duchy under the Danish crown, and the language conditions of any subject will be respected. Yet the confidence in the King's impartiality is undiminished.*[28]

Christian VIII's efforts to retain the absolute power and unity of the autocratic monarchy in Denmark came too late. His predecessor, Frederik VI, reform processes and the growing desire for sovereignty, liberalization, and democratization had become part of the political mentality of the Danish population, a development that had gone faster than even what the absolute monarchy could control. Christian VIII's reign

[25] Jens Gunni Busck, *Christian 8: konge af først Norge og siden Danmark* (Copenhagen: Historika: in collaboration with The Royal Danish Collection, 2015).

[26] Henning Dehn-Nielsen, *Christian 8: konge af Danmark, konge af Norge* (Copenhagen: Sesam, 1999).

[27] Danish-Norwegian priest and poet Casper Johannes Boye (1791–1853).

[28] Christian VIII, & Anders Monrad Møller. *Kong Christian VIII.s Dagbøger og Optegnelser*, Vol. 4. Pt. 1, 1839–1843 (Copenhagen: Det Kongelige Danske Selskab for Fædrelandets Historie, 1995).

was short; he died of blood poisoning as a result of a bloodletting in 1848, and in his political will to his son, the future King Frederik VII (1843–1912),[29] he reluctantly encouraged the need for a swift and free Danish constitution.[30] The year 1848 is well-known as the great European Revolutionary year. In France, the revolution broke out in February, which—again—abolished the French monarchy and established the Second French Republic; in March, the liberal uprisings kicked off in Germany with the citizens demanding more political freedom, more democracy, less censorship, and more openness—a popular protest that resonated in countries such as Denmark and Sweden, where the bourgeoisie in particular demanded free constitutions and a fundamental change in the governing systems.[31]

In Denmark, the "revolution" was calmer than other European examples. As early as January 1848, the new Danish king, Frederik VII, chose to lift significant restrictions on freedom of the press and reform the rights of Estate Assemblies in a more democratic direction.[32] The abolition of the freedom of the press led to an increased political debate and in March, the craftsman's movement, and Society of the Friends of Peasants (Danish: Bondevennernes Selskab), led by the National Liberals' Orla Lehmann (1810–1870), gathered in a popular petition demanding once and for all, a free constitution.[33] King Frederik VII could do nothing but meet the demands of the crowd, and thus dismissed his royally appointed cabinet of ministers in favor of a temporary administration, the so-called March Ministry, consisting of prominent figures from the rebellious popular movement. The March Ministry was given the task of writing a draft of a Danish constitution, which could subsequently be adopted by a democratically elected Constitutional Assembly.[34]

[29] With the telling royal motto of "The love of the people, (is) my strength".

[30] Dehn-Nielsen, *Christian 8: konge af Danmark, konge af Norge.*

[31] John M. Merriman, *A History of Modern Europe: From the Renaissance to the Present* (New York: W.W. Norton, 1996).

[32] Claus Bjørn, *1848: borgerkrig og revolution*, 2. ed. (Copenhagen: Gyldendal, 1999).

[33] Hans Vammen, "Casino 48", *Historisk Tidsskrift*, 88:2 (1988), pp. 253–281. See also Orla Lehmann & Hother Hage, *Orla Lehmanns efterladte Skrifter*, Vol. 2. (Copenhagen: Gyldendal, 1873).

[34] L.K.D Frederik Barfod, *Den grundlovgivende Rigsforsamlings Historie, kortelig fortalt af L.K.D* (Copenhagen: Forfatterens Forlag, 1849). For the March Ministry, also known as Regeringen Molkte I, see also Regeringen, "Regeringen Molkte I: 22. marts

A year later, on June 5, 1849, the June constitution the first Danish constitution, was adopted by the Constitutional Assembly. The June constitution made Denmark a constitutional monarchy and the constitution secured a number of freedoms such as: freedom of speech, freedom of the press, freedom of association, and freedom of assembly.[35] By modern standards, the June constitution can hardly be described as widespread democratic, as large sections of the population still would not have the right to vote among them: women, servants, poor, insane, criminals, foreigners, and men without their own household under 30 years of age.[36] These voting restrictions were first lifted some 65 years later in 1915.[37]

The Freedom of Trade Act and Impacts of the Danish Freedom Reforms

What constitutes a free society? Is it the state's ability to protect the rights of its citizens, or a citizen's right to transform and organize the state in a manner, so that the state itself cannot threaten the rights of these citizen? The role of the state and government vs. the rights of its citizens, were one of the decisive political questions in the years following the introduction of the Danish constitution. In the period 1849 until 1863, Danish politics was divided into two main political movements. The first was the liberal movement, the one based on a somewhat libertarian and age of enlightenment mindset, that had ensured a free constitution and wanted the role, power, and influence of the state and government, often restricting the lives of its citizens, to be diminished. For the liberal movement, the freedom of the citizen was the most crucial.[38]

At the other end of the political spectrum was the conservative movement and its approach to the role and function of the state. The conservative movement, to a large extent, wanted the preservation of the

1848–16. November 1848", *Regeringen*, https://www.regeringen.dk/om-regeringen/regeringer-siden-1848/regeringen-moltke-i/, Accessed Jan 24, 2021.

[35] Den grundlovgivende rigsforsamling, "Danmarks Riges Grundlov, 5. juni 1849", *Departementstidende* (5 June 1849), p. 489.

[36] Bertel Nygaard, *Grundloven* (Aarhus: Aarhus Universitetsforlag, 2017).

[37] Anette Faye Jacobsen, *Ulige rettigheder* (Aarhus: Aarhus Universitetsforlag, 2021).

[38] Bertel Nygaard, "Demokratibegrebets gennembrud i Danmark 1848", *Historisk Tidsskrift*, 111:1 (2011), pp. 37–73.

social order, as known before the introduction of the constitution. The conservative movement was also fundamentally democratic-minded, albeit a bit skeptical of democracy as a form of government. The most important thing for the conservative movement was the preservation of the (constitutional) monarchy, as well as the preservation of some indirect privileges and rights of the ancient feudal nobility, which stood in contrast to the liberal approach.[39]

The fundamental question that separated the two movements, the liberals and the conservatives, was the question of the future of the Helstat.[40] While Danish politicians drafted the elements of the constitution in 1848–1849, a revolt had occurred in the Danish-German duchies, as the German-speaking population in the duchies of Schleswig and Holstein, wanted to secede from Denmark.[41] The uprising developed into an all out civil war, the First Schleswig War (1848–1850), which later also gained a more international character, when Prussia chose to support the German-speaking insurgents from Schleswig–Holstein. The war ended with a status quo, and the duchies remained part of the Danish possessions and thus the Helstat-structure remained intact.[42]

The point of contention between the two movements, after the end of the war in 1850, was the question of the status of the duchies in the Danish Helstat. The liberal movement, at that point of time championed by the *National-Liberal* party, wanted to integrate the predominantly Danish-speaking duchy of Schleswig to Denmark. In return, the National-Liberals wanted the predominantly German-speaking duchies of Holstein and Lauenburg, were to be left to the German Confederation. The

[39] Palle Svensson, "Var vore forfatningsfædre demokratiske?", *Temp*, no. 5 (2012), pp. 5–27; See also Claus Friisberg, "Var Junigrundloven demokratisk? Et svar til Palle Svensson", *Temp*, no. 6 (2013), pp. 158–169.

[40] Ove Korsgaard, *Kampen om folket: et dannelsesperspektiv på dansk historie gennem 500 år* (Copenhagen: Gyldendal, 2004).

[41] Jens Ahlers & Jan Schlürmann, *Aufbruch & Bürgerkrieg. Schleswig–Holstein 1848–1851*, Vol. 1–2 (Kiel: Schleswig-Holsteinische Landesbibliothek, 2012).

[42] Niels Peder Jensen, *Den første slesvigske Krig 1848–50* (Copenhagen: Vilhelm Trydes Forlag, 1898/2012).

conservative movement, represented by the party *Højre*, wanted something different, their aim was to maintain the status quo that was the result of the peace negotiations after the First Schleswig War.[43]

While Denmark and Danish politics in the 1850s in particular were marked by the Helstat-question, Danish politicians, predominantly politicians from the National-Liberal party, carried out extensive reforms aimed at liberating, what only a few years prior had been monarchist subjects, the now democratic citizens. During these years, extensive reforms were implemented in, for example, the educational area and the church area.[44] Among other things, forced baptism was abolished and the citizens were set free to choose their own priest and congregation, thereby effectively expanding the Danish freedom of religion initiated in Danish constitution, which since the Danish Reformation in 1536 had been strongly orthodox and periodically pietistic.[45] In the area of schools and education, conditions were also improved, among other things by including private actors and benefactors, and in general, individual educational institutions were given a freer framework and conditions for running the education system.[46]

Of the many liberal reforms and laws from the period, I would like to highlight a special piece of legislation which I would argue is the most important piece of Danish legislation in the mid-nineteenth century constitutional period, in many ways both more important and, at least in practice, more liberating, than the Danish constitution, namely the *Freedom of Trade Act* of 1857 (Danish: Næringsfrihedsloven). The Freedom of Trade Act is particularly essential, as it is a break from several hundred-year-old institutions, which for as long as they had existed, had been a hindrance to the free functioning of the Danish citizens/subjects. The Freedom of Trade Act was passed in 1857 and fully implemented in 1861, and its significance for Danish development and prosperity is

[43] Lorenz Rerup, "Fra litterær til politisk nationalisme", In: Ole Feldbæk, *Dansk identitetshistorie*, Vol. 2 (Copenhagen: C.A. Reitzel, 1991).

[44] Michael Bregnsbo, *Samfundsorden og statsmagt set fra prædikestolen: danske præsters deltagelse i den offentlige opinionsdannelse vedrørende samfundsordenen og statsmagten 1750–1848, belyst ved trykte prædikener: en politisk-idéhistorisk undersøgelse* (Copenhagen, Det Kongelige Bibliotek, 1997).

[45] Feldbæk, "Den lange fred".

[46] Hans Vammen, *Den tomme stat: angst og ansvar i dansk politik 1848–1864* (Copenhagen: Museum Tusculanum, 2011).

one I regard second to none. With the adoption of the law, all restrictions on the individual's freedom of choice, in relation to the choice of work and trade, were effectively removed. Mercantilism was abolished for free-market economics.[47]

As described, what had been a working guideline for centuries, namely that the bakers' son became a baker's apprentice, and the blacksmith's son had to involuntary agree to follow his father's and grandfather's work in the same forge and anvil, in the same village or town—regardless of whether he himself, or other members of the generations of blacksmiths, bakers, etc., had the ability, will, or desire for the craft. Thus, for centuries, one had been bound to a profession which one could only avoid by costly trials. The Freedom of Trade Act also abolished the rights of the privileged market towns. Danish privileged market towns were a type of city, in most cases founded in the Middle Ages, to which the royal power had granted special privileges. These privileges often meant that the city had the exclusive right to craft and trade within a particular area, a right to independent administration, their own legal and judiciary system, exemptions from certain taxes and an exemption from conscription.[48] At the beginning of the nineteenth century, there were 66 privileged market towns in Denmark, and they were in many ways comparable to the German Hanseatic cities, where the peasants in the rural catchment areas of these cities were characterized by very limited, if not lacking the rights that could be found within the city walls. The privileged market town-system was a product of a deeply mercantilist culture, which mentioned earlier had its origins in the Danish and European Middle Ages, and thus one of the concrete obstacles to the liberal movement's desire to accelerate free trade, innovation, and equal civil rights in the land-city divide.[49]

The adoption of liberal freedom reforms, such as the Freedom of Trade Act, raises an obvious question, namely how the National-Liberals could have such comprehensive reforms implemented, at a time when the free trade-oriented, and somewhat libertarian political groupings did not hold an absolute majority in either the Danish House of Commons (Danish:

[47] Hansen, "Økonomisk vækst i Danmark: 1720–1914".

[48] Henrik Gade Jensen, *Menneskekærlighedens værk: det danske civilsamfund før velfærdsstaten* (Copenhagen: CEPOS, 2011).

[49] Ronit, "Handelens vej er altid kulturens vej, Det Danske Handelskammer 1742–1992".

Folketinget) or the House of Lords (Danish: Landstinget). As I pointed out in the introduction to this chapter, the traditional interpretation of the period of the Danish civil rights and freedom reforms has been characterized by a tendency toward a harmonized, consensual, and linear history writing. Here, the period from the adoption of the constitution in 1849 to outbreak of the Second Schleswig War in 1864 is shaped as a period characterized by progressive political support widespread throughout the Danish political spectrum.[50]

I will, in contrary to the harmonized interpretation of the period, put forward an antithesis that the National-Liberals succeeded in carrying out such extensive reforms, as it promoted the efforts of the conservative party Højre, in areas of (1) centralization of the state and (2) increasing the tax base. These moves would later make the redistributive welfare state a possibility.

The abolition of privileges also meant that the citizens of the privileged market towns lost the special degree of autonomy, of which many of the cities and their inhabitants had enjoyed since the Middle Ages. This was indisputably a case of a centralization of state power. Thereby the market town bourgeois was now subject to governmental and parliamentary decrees, legislation, state administration, and control, which previously was handled locally at the city hall. Thus, the citizens of the privileged market towns had less influence on their own everyday lives after the reforms, a trend which only increased during the nineteenth and twentieth centuries. The general liberal movement initially promoted the need to introduce equal civil rights between the citizens of the rural hinterland and the privileged market towns. But it led to a costly centralization of the state on behalf of the influence of bourgeois democracy in privileged market towns, which in some cases had existed for centuries.

In addition to the increased centralization, the freedom reforms also invoked a restructuring of the tax base of the privileged market towns, and the revenues on their trade, commerce, and crafts. After the transition to autocratic monarchy in 1660, the first major records of Danish cadastre-maps (Danish: Matrikel-kort) were introduced by King Frederik III in 1662.[51] The cadastre-maps were a state record of peasants and

[50] Fellman et al., *Creating Nordic Capitalism: The Business History of a Competitive Periphery*.

[51] Erik Alstrup & Poul Erik Olsen, *Dansk kulturhistorisk opslagsværk* (Copenhagen: Dansk Historisk Fællesforening, 1991).

landowners' property outside the privileged market towns, established in order record an overview of property taxation and assessments of the semi-annual tax revenues, based on estimates of landowners' dividends. During the seventeenth, eighteenth, and nineteenth centuries, the Danish cadastre-maps were continuously reformed and tax regulations expanded from the amount of grain a farmer could cultivate, to valuations and taxation of uncultivated fields, forests, and meadows.[52] Until 1857, with the implementation of the Freedom of Trade Act, the privileged market towns had been exempt from taxation through cadastre. The new legislation changed this, which meant that citizens in the privileged market towns now had to pay compared to earlier new and relatively to before, high property taxes directly to the state at the same time as the introduction of a state tax on the income of the urban industries.

Increased state taxation on the urban occupations of the privileged market towns was not the initial intention of the liberal movement, with the far-reaching freedom reforms. Taxation via cadastre had in meantime become a regular necessity for the continuation of the state, whose primary expenditure in the second half of the nineteenth century was the Danish military, navy, and defense in general. The reason for the need to expand the cadastre taxation was the cessation of one of Denmark's largest sources of income, the Sound Tolls (Danish: Øresundstolden). The Sound Tolls was a transit custom on maritime trade and transit in the Danish belts and the Sound (Danish: Øresund) and had since its introduction in the thirteenth century onward been one of the country's most important sources of income. During the eighteenth century, the seafaring nations had paid the Sound Toll tariffs without much protest, and the number of ships paying the tariffs increased steadily throughout the century from approx. 2500 in 1720 to over 12,000 ships around the year 1800.[53]

The increased maritime trade of the nineteenth century began to voice critical concerns about the Danish Sound Toll, which had become so expensive for maritime trading nations, that in many cases it was cheaper to transport its goods over land from Hamburg to Lübeck, to avoid the high Danish tariffs. In 1855, the United States declared, that it would

[52] Trond Bjerkås, "Et Nytt Blikk På Befolkningen? - Om 1723-Matrikkelens Konsekvenser Og Årsakene Til Dens Fall", *Heimen*, no. 2 (2014), pp. 126–143.

[53] Ole Degn, *Tolden i Sundet: toldopkrævning, politik og skibsfart i Øresund 1429–1857* (Copenhagen: Told- og Skattehistorisk Selskab, 2010).

no longer submit to the Danish tariffs, a declaration to which several major maritime trading nations agreed. The US declaration led to negotiations between Denmark, the United States, and several of the important seafaring nations, whereby an agreement was reached on the abolition of the Sound Toll in 1857.[54] In return, Denmark gained a one-time compensation of 10.5 million dollars, which corresponded to approx. 12 years of tax revenue.[55]

On the one hand, the freedom reforms were undeniably positive for Denmark, especially the Freedom of Trade Act which dismantled the age-old Danish mercantilism, and replaced it with free-market competition and opened up for innovation and the Great Enrichment,[56] which were great gains for the general Danish citizen both in terms of rights and prosperity, and in particular for and fuelled by the early Danish business firms, as described in more detail in Chapter 5.

On the other hand, with this interpretation of the motives for the Danish freedom reforms in the middle of the nineteenth century, I find that willingness to reform were less marked by the often emphasized Danish liberal idealism of the period, on the contrary, much of the liberal reform should be seen as elements of conservative pragmatism. I argue that the conservative movement, and especially the conservative party 'Højre', did not see democratization and liberalization as an end-goal in itself like the National-Liberals and liberal movement, but more as a means of creating a sustainable tax base and a stable effective state for Denmark through the mechanisms of free-market trade and competition.

In January 1864, the Danish National-Liberal government rejected a Prussian-Austrian ultimatum to repeal the Danish constitution, which states that Schleswig–Holstein was a part of Denmark. The Danish rejection is part of the National-Liberals' base policy, of the full annexation of Schleswig into Denmark, as previously described in this chapter. The war of 1864, also known as the Second Schleswig War, became a national

[54] Erik Gøbel, "Øresundstolden Og Dens Regnskaber 1497–1857", *M/S Museet for Søfarts årbog*, no. 69 (2010), pp. 41–72.

[55] Brazil, one of the maritime nations that was to contribute to the Danish compensation, never made its payment to the Danish state. Only during the Brazilian President Luiz Inacio Lula da Silva's state visit to Denmark in 2007, the Danish Prime Minister and later NATO-Secretary General, Anders Fogh Rasmussen, in a symbolic act, forgave the 152-year-old Brazilian debt.

[56] McCloskey, "Liberalism—Caused the Modern World".

disaster and tragedy for Denmark. The war ended with a Danish relinquishment of the German duchies and has since been regarded as the foremost example of the hubris of the National-Liberals and the liberal movement, which after the end of the war lost most of its political support among the Danish population.

The Conservative Counter-Movement

Denmark's defeat in the Second Schleswig War changed not only Denmark's geographical landscape, but also the political one. The conservative party Højre took power, and implemented a revised constitution in 1866, which re-established the King's right to personally select the Danish government. The revised constitution also entailed a privileged suffrage for the Danish House of Lords, comprised by estate owners and landlords, which mainly supported Højre. The opposition in the House of Commons wanted to introduce parliamentarism, so it was the people and not the king, who appointed the government.[57] For several years, Denmark underwent a major constitutional struggle, in which the conservative party Højre remained in power, against the will of the people, and stubbornly maintained, that the king, who was himself a supporter of a conservative government, had the right to elect the government, regardless of the fact, that the population did not support the government in repeated elections.[58]

With the king's support, the conservative Højre governments remained in office under the leadership of Prime Minister Jacob Brønnum Scavenius Estrup (1825–1913), and from 1885 until 1894, Denmark was de facto subject to a conservative dictatorship.[59] In no small way in response to a failed assignation attempt on the prime minister, and the growing local gun clubs and liberal volunteer forces demanding liberal reforms, as well as increased unionizing among workers. Estrup's administration imposed new taxes on citizens' incomes and wealth, and set up a state

[57] Lorenz Rerup, *Danmarks historie: Tiden 1864–1914*, Søren Mørch (ed.), Vol. 6 (Copenhagen: Gyldendal, 1992).

[58] Vagn Dybdahl, John Danstrup, Hal Koch, Erik Kjersgaard, & Svend Cedergreen Bech, *Danmarks historie*: *De nye klasser 1870–1913*, Vol. 12, 3. ed. (Copenhagen: Politiken, 1978).

[59] Ditlev Tamm, *Konseilspræsidenten: Jacob Brønnum Scavenius Estrup: 1825–1913* (Copenhagen: Gyldendal, 1996).

intelligence corps, that acted on direct orders and in the interests of the Estrup administration.[60] Throughout period, known as *Provisorie-tiden*, the Højre-government continuously deviated from the democratic foundations of the constitution, despite the opposition of the Danish population. After Estrup resigned as Prime Minister, the major opposition party *Venstre* gained power, and introduced parliamentarism in 1901. However, due to the limited economic size of the state, industry still flourished and expanded.[61]

Conclusion

It is partly on the basis of Estrup's administration, Denmark's only dictatorship, that I find it difficult to reconcile myself with the usual harmonized narrative about the origins of the Danish welfare state. Many of the state structures left by Estrup, including the increased taxes, were in most cases maintained by the subsequent governments and as a result of Danish neutrality policy during and after World War I, the expenditure on the Danish military was greatly reduced, and later used to support the first major state welfare programs of the 1930s.

The reasons for the conservative support for the liberalization of free trade and general the freedom of the people, stated in the freedom reforms as the Freedom of Trade Act, can and should be interpreted, as being part of filling the coffers to meet other policy goals, rather than the widely held narrative of a consensual desire to liberate citizens—which originally were only the goals of the Danish liberal movements, with their extensive reforms of the 1840s and 1850s.

[60] Troels Fink, *Estruptidens politiske historie 1875–1894* (Odense: Odense Universitets-forlag, 1986).

[61] Thomsen, "Industri, stat og samfund, 1870–1939".

CHAPTER 3

Danish Economic Policy and Institutions in the Twentieth Century: From Laisse Fair to a Mixed Economy?

Towards a New Dominant Institutional Logic

Institutions have been argued to follow logics that compete for dominance. This process, as competition more generally, is dynamic and rarely settled. Mostly a nation stays in one dominant logic which can be interacted upon by proponents of competing logics.[1] The institutional logic's interplay is historically different across nations, producing country-level institutionalized logics that are unique.[2] The actual manifestation of institutional logics touches on the pillars of state, market, and society. Institutional logic is the combination of the pillars of society, state, and market to generate one of four types of national economies or logics: a liberal type promoting market dominance, a social rights type that sets social limits to market strategies, a developmental type in which market strategies are coordinated by the state and society, and a socialist type in

[1] Patricia H. Thornton, Michael Lounsbury, & William Ocasio, *The Institutional Logics Perspective: A New Approach to Culture, Structure, and Process* (Oxford: Oxford University Press, 2012).

[2] Seán Ó Riain, "States and Markets in an Era of Globalization", *Annual Review of Sociology*, 26:1 (2000), pp. 187–213.

© The Author(s), under exclusive license to Springer Nature Switzerland AG 2022

S. K. Sløk-Madsen, *Danish Capitalism in the 20th Century*, Palgrave Studies in Economic History,
https://doi.org/10.1007/978-3-031-04267-6_3

which the state seeks to retain power and to subsume market and society.[3] What is fundamentally interesting for Denmark in the twentieth century is that we see a change of logic from liberal to social.[4]

By far, the biggest lasting institutional change for Denmark in the twentieth century was the transition from a strong, but small state to a vast universal welfare state. With such a strong conclusion, the chapter sets out to explain how that happened and what it meant for business, politics, and citizens of Denmark. In fact, Denmark's status as a mixed economy is largely traceable to this development. Prior to the welfare state, regulatory efficiency was high, but the size of the state was small. It is also important to comment upfront on an often misunderstood aspect of mixed economies, namely that they are always welfare states. That is not a requirement for a mixed economy. A mixed economy is merely one with significant elements of both state and market, precisely what the government priorities are, is a separate political matter. In the case of Denmark, we can observe that the motivation for redistribution and state-owned welfare production also changed toward the end of the twentieth century, manifesting completely in the twenty-first century.

It is important to note that the version of history presented in this chapter is but one way—by far the most dominant and prevalent today—to think about the Danish welfare state. In this chapter, the Danish universal welfare state is presented as a business model employed by the state with not only massive redistribution, but also close to the monopolistic production of welfare services. Yet that does not have to be the case. Most modern states have elements of welfare statism, but their exact scope and implementation is very different from the one we see in Denmark. Likewise, the notion that the general national community has a role to play in the difficulties of individual life is not an exclusively modern phenomenon either. Far back in history, we can trace both state and voluntary welfare measures whereby the community helped individuals, especially those less fortunate or who had fallen on bad times.

Therefore, it is also important to remember, that the state is not required for individuals to generate prosperity through communities to

[3] Neil J. Smelser & Richard Swedberg (eds.), *The Handbook of Economic Sociology* (Princeton: Princeton University Press: 2010).

[4] Nevers, *Det produktive samfund: seks kapitler af industrialiseringens idéhistorie.*

other individuals. Throughout the Western world, and probably also outside it, there are examples of voluntary joint associations that have provided joint assistance in the form of savings, joint purchases of medicine and medical care, and support in the event of unemployment, deaths, and the like. Some of these have been founded around religious communities, working communities, locality or other things that naturally bound people together.[5] It can be recommended to read *Menneskekærlighedens Værk* by Henrik Gade Jensen for a closer investigation into how welfare goods were provided in Denmark before the welfare state we know today.[6] When I nevertheless describe the creation of the modern Danish welfare state as it is, it is thus not to highlight it as something normatively better or unique, but simply a purely methodical choice, as it is the institutional arrangements Danes ended up living in after the twentieth century and as a consequence of it.

The Important Scandals and Life Before the Welfare State

As stated in Chapter 1, the start of the twentieth century in Denmark is the socalled System Change of 1901 where modern Danish parliamentarism took hold, cemented with universal suffrage in 1915, and with the final victory of parliamentarism or monarchy in the 1920 Easter Crisis.

Politically, the traditional two parties gave way to a growing number of alternative parties over the twentieth century,[7] where the first major development was the steep rise in popularity for the social democratic movement,[8] particularly at the cost of Venstre. The party "Venstre", fragmented, and from it emerged "Radikale Venstre", so that now there was two parties. Højre after some initial disruptions became the Conservative People's Party. The extremes were also present with the foundation of

[5] Pierson & Castles, *The Welfare State Reader*; Palmer, *After the Welfare State: Politicians Stole Your Future... You Can Get It Back.*

[6] Jensen, *Menneskekærlighedens værk – Det danske civilsamfund før velfærdsstaten.*

[7] As of writing, the number of parties for the next parliamentary election will be 13. Not counting the North Atlantic mandates, there are 14 different groups currently in parliament. Up from 8 in 2001.

[8] 46% in the 1935 election. The Social-Democratic party was the leading government party from 1929 to 1940.

the Danish Communist Party in 1920 and the Danish National Socialist Movement in 1930, and even a center-georgist party Retsforbundet.

It was also during the twentieth century that Denmark and the Danish Commonwealth (Rigsfællesskabet) would arrive at its modern shape. While defense issues in the period from 1901 to 1940 was a main point of contention between the parties, the dispute was not neutrality. What was debated was the path to neutrality. One side argued Denmark should maintain a strong army to defend its independence, but not a force large enough to pose a threat to anyone, particularly Germany, while the other side argued for versions of disarmament. Neutrality was maintained in World War I and rather than using the opportunity to reclaim all of the lost territory from the 1864 defeat, a referendum was held, and the border drawn according to majority sympathies in the local counties. The process of unification completed in 1920. Furthermore, the possessions in the West Indies were sold to the United States in 1917, and in 1918 Iceland became independent, but agreed to remain in the Commonwealth for 25 years, which lasted untill 1944.

Denmark was part of the Scandinavian monetary union from the beginning of the twentieth century.[9] The union, as well as the gold standard, was dissolved at the advent of World War I. Later attempts at reintroducing the monetary union was met with fierce resistance and it remained dead. The gold standard did however remerge in 1925 and lasted untill 1931 where it was abolished once again, as the Danish krone had seen a series of devaluations due to the main British export market abandonment of the standard.

The period leading up to global depression of the 1930s was generally a period of growing prosperity and rising industry, with agriculture remaining both the main employer and exporter, however a declining one in the period.[10] GDP, measured in fixed prices, tripled and relatively speaking the average Danes were among the world's most prosperous per capita. Despite industry was growing, but politically Denmark's chances as an industrial power in its own right was doubted due to the lack of natural resources.[11] However, new innovations were adopted by an

[9] Each Scandinavian country maintained their own currency, but they were usable in all three countries.

[10] Thomsen, "Industri, stat og samfund, 1870–1939".

[11] Dybdahl et al., *Danmarks historie: De nye klasser 1870–1913*.

increasingly affluent consumer base. Most noticeable was the car. Ford Motor Company even established a factory in Denmark, roads were expanded, and cities changed to make way for this innovation.[12]

Generally speaking, the economic policy of the time did not influence the economic conditions much, but was more reactive in nature. It is questionable if the dominant liberal institutional logic of the time was a policy choice, or just taken as the natural order of things. It was certainly put on a pause at the outbreak of World War I and replaced by a command-oriented economic policy. A return to the liberal logic was initiated after, but by the advent of the global crises of 1929, the foreign trade system was in free fall. Instead, the countries agreed to two-sided trade agreements on a quid pro quo basis. The dominance of the agricultural interest showed its hands in these measures and forced the import allotment over to English products as this was the main export market for the sector. In an attempt to limit import generally, non-Danish agricultural goods were again the main target, where nuts would, for the next 100 years, have specific tariffs, while potato-based products, including unhealthy variants, were subsidized.

In 1932, the state created *Valutacentralen*—the currency central exchange—to control the import. Industry quickly got an active part to play in relation to the private trade organizations controlling distribution of import permits. It was a result of a well-established tradition where trade and industry organizations, and from 1920, unions as well, would be invited to advise on economic policy in commissions and boards. The approach to policy development and implementation was not based on democratic coherence as one might be led to believe, but rather an attempt to limit the state apparatus. Whether that worked is a matter for sore debate—Valutacentralen ended up having as many employees as the entire central state administration itself.

Labor conflict was on the rise in the early twentieth century, particularly after World War I. Trade union membeships doubled, and several workers' rights were established such as an 8 hour workday and summer vacation. While the real wage fluctuated with the times, the working-class conflict-readiness fell and a national compromise became more

[12] Michael F. Wagner, *Domesticeringen af Ford i Danmark: Den kulturelle tilegnelse af Ford og fordismen, 1920–1940*, Paper presented at Det amerikanske forbillede? Amerikanisering, erhverv, teknologi og organisationer (Denmark: Syddansk Universitet, 2009); Martin Zerlang, *Danmark set gennem en bilrude* (Copenhagen: Gads forlag, 2021).

clear; the workers had their eyes on middle-class living, and businesses wanted to avoid too much state interference. An important contributor was the 1907 establishment of unemployment schemes organized by the trade unions, but supported in part by the state and employers too. This incentivizes union members to stay in unions during periods of unemployment, but was an individual insurance scheme, like health insurance (Danish: Sygekasser), not general or state-based welfare program.[13] It cemented a strong organization of both workers and employers.

Technological adaptation was welcomed and accelerating in all fields from industry to entertainment. Electricity became widespread and close to ubiquitous by the outbreak of World War II, including increased adaptation of electric machinery and appliances in both industry and at home. The growing popularity of cars put an end to the expansion of the railroad, and instead improvement of roads became the main priority. Trains remained important for transportation of goods and the period saw significant reduction in intercity travel times for particular trains. As for personal transportation, the bicycle quickly went from sport equitment to used for everyday transport by the masses, busses, and electric trams also counted for local transport needs. Technology, consumer demand, and regulation changed the cityscape, but buildings in three stories was the most popular, as they did not require cranes to build, which meant that even the larger towns grew in square miles, more so than in height.

Information was spread rapidly, but was somewhat controlled by state-run agencies and most newspapers officially aligning with a specific political party. Phones also grew in popularity, again, both privately and professionally. Educational reform was initiated with larger schools, both for intellectual pursuits, and specialist schools for vocational activities. However, implementation was limited before the end of World War II.

[13] Skyum-Nielsen, *Arveguldet - Danskernes Værdier.*

Banking Crisis and Shift of Sentiments

Important to mention is also two very prominent banking scandals. The first classical liberal government under Prime Minister I.C. Christensen (1858–1930) was hit by a major scandal when the justice minister P. A. Alberti (1851–1932) was found guilty in a case concerning embezzlement. Alberti was a flamboyant character and banker. He suffered from ludomania and was likely attracted to politics to combat his increasingly tarnished commercial reputation. While admittedly a capable political talent, he was also authoritarian and somewhat old-fashioned compared to the rest of Venstre, which was the party he represented. He was forced to resign in 1908 and later turned himself in for embezzlement of 18 million DKK (1.2 billion DKK as of 2020) for which he was convicted and sentenced to eight years of hard labor imprisonment. One of the immediate results of the case was an impeachment trial for the Prime Minister of which he was acquitted, but from which his reputation never fully recovered. The case—internationally famous at the time—more importantly further contributed to a growing skepticism of the tenants of "high capitalism", finance, urbanization, and growth.[14]

Further fuel to this ideological fire was given by another banking scandal roughly a decade later. The Danish financial institution Landmandsbanken (the farmer's bank) had become the largest in Scandinavia, but to the surprise of most had to be restructured in September of 1922, and the state had to underwrite it in February 1923. It was a surprise only to the public however as the bank with the expressed blessing of both the national bank and the government had dismissed the seriousness of the crisis in the months prior to the bust. The dire strait of the bank was in large part due to providing debt capital to risky ventures, like Det Transatlantiske Kompagni, and others particularly doing World War I.

This case again was further fuel to an ideological rift concerning the role of growth and entrepreneurship in wealth creation, and when the global financial markets crashed in 1929, a bank law was passed requiring banks to hold larger reserves, which helped Denmark avoid any bank failures as a result of this crisis, however it did potentially hinder innovation and investment in the years to come. Ideologically, the Danish embraced

[14] Boje, *Vejen til velstand–marked, stat og utopi: Hvorfor blev Danmark rigt–og ikke rigere? Tiden 1850–1930.*

the satirical Law of Jante where the mediocre is the aim of life. To the later outspoken frustration of many businessmen, Denmark in the twentieth century was to aim small in all matters, expect for the size of the state. The conclusion was yet another manifestation of the Danish compromise. Now in the ultimate formulation, Danish market economy could likely exist without the state, but would only be allowed to do so by and for the state.

The English Inspiration

At the beginning of the post-World War I period, only Switzerland had as limited a public sector as Denmark. The country's prosperity at that time continued to depend to a large extent on an extreme commercial specialization in the production of agricultural products. This made it obvious to choose a liberal model of society, as this allows professions to specialize and promotes free innovation.

There had, of course, been cyclical movements, but the first fundamental blow to agricultural-based growth came with the international economic downturn that followed the stock market crash in the United States in 1929. Suddenly, Danish agricultural exports, which predominantly went to the UK, were threatened, and soon it got worse. At the collapse of the international payment system virtually all countries initiated direct foreign trade restrictions. A significant consequence was a marked increase in unemployment, from 14% in 1930 to 32% in 1933.

In that situation, a new crisis policy saw the light of day carried by the Social Democratic party and the Danish Social-Liberal Party (Radikale Venstre), which took over government power from a Venstre minority government in 1929 and maintained it right up until the outbreak of World War II. The focal point was the Kanslergade Settlement in 1933, where social and labor market policy was decisively renewed and strengthened, and where a political agreement was created to develop a higher degree of state control of foreign trade to ensure the best possible use of scarce foreign currency. Another outcome was a national alignment of welfare and social transfers which benefited recipients in rural areas, but disadvantaged recipients in larger towns. Likewise, public sector activity increased from an employment point of view by initiating large-scale construction work and by strengthening the municipalities' finances so that the unemployed could be supported and schools, etc., could be expanded. There is a strong myth today that the welfare state was planned and the Kanslergade Settlement was a kind of Danish social triumph: a birth certificate for the later universal welfare state. It should be emphasized, however, that the Kanslergade Settlement was an expression of a crisis situation, and as such not heroic or visionary foresight.[15]

It would therefore be a mistake to regard the crisis policy of the 1930s as a real recognition of a modern welfare state. The new social policy continued to be based on need assessment, and social assistance still depended on the *cause* of the need. In the view of both the state and the general public, a social service recipient was either a person worthy of need fallen on hard times (værdigt trængende) or the more common unworthy needy (uværdigt trængende). Both groups could receive help, but civil rights, including the right to vote, could in principle be revoked for those deemed unworthy of need as a penalty for their burden on society. Sure, public spending saw some growth, but under-budgeting as a matter of principle and fiscal thinking had not really taken hold. However, in the 1930s, there was an interest among new younger economists, such as Poul Nyboe Andersen (1913–2004), Erik Ib Schmidt (1911–1998), Jørgen Dich (1901–1975), and Viggo Kampmann (1910–1976), in new ideas that had been developed in the UK in previous years. This generation of economist, the social engineers, would go on to hold not only academic positions but civil service jobs and also political offices—Kampmann even became Prime Minister.[16] Their interest in command economy grew during the war years, and thus the intellectual foundation for a breakthrough for a welfare state after 1945 was cast. Besides the small, but growing interest in the ideas of Keynes (1883–1946), William Beveridge (1879–1963) was a key inspirator for the aspiring young economist. He was socially oriented economist who developed the notion of a universal welfare state that included universal social security for all citizens with the 1942 report Social Insurance and Allied Services, commissioned by the British War Cabinet and translated

[15] Erik Rasmussen, *Danmarks historie: Velfærdsstaten på vej. 1913–1939*, Vol. 13, John Danstrup, & Hal Koch (eds.) (Copenhagen: Politikens Forlag, 1978).

[16] Erik Ib Schmidt, *Dansk økonomisk politik: Danmarks Radios grundbøger* (Copenhagen: Det Kongelige Bibliotek, 1959); Erik Ib Schmidt & Jørgen Teytaud, *Fra psykopatklubben: erindringer og optegnelser* (Copenhagen: Gyldendal Lydbøger, 1995); Poul Smidt, *Viggo Kampmann: modig modstandsmand, klog finansminister, ustyrlig statsminister* (Copenhagen: Gyldendal, 2016); Arne Hardis, *Den kætterske socialdemokrat: Jørgen Dich og den herskende klasse* (Copenhagen: Gyldendal, 2018).

into social reform immediately after 1945.[17] With the book Citizenship and Social Class from 1950, the sociologist TH Marshall presented the notion of "citizenship rights", which should be unconditionally given by virtue of citizenship itself as different from early civil rights ideals, where social rights were correlated with political rights. Every citizen should be guaranteed civil, political, and social rights no matter their circumstances. The welfare state should be universal.[18]

These ideas came to put a decisive imprint on the development of Danish society in the late 1940s and in the 1950s. When a Social Democratic government took office in 1947, it established a Ministry of Economic Affairs with an Economic Secretariat with the task of developing macroeconomic planning and governance in Denmark.[19] This new different approach to citizen rights became binding law with the constitution of 1953, which abolished the Landsting (the two chamber system) and saw political power equally divided between citizens. The universality of social rights got the definitive breakthrough with the tax-financed national pension in 1956. The conclusion was that Denmark, again contrary to many people's belief, does not have a true threefold division of power, and in reality is an almost totally, often narrow, majority government ruling in an intellectual climate that favored expansive fiscal policy and worried little about budget deficits or the political incentives later pointed out by the public choice tradition.[20]

[17] William Beveridge, *Social Insurance and Allied Services* (London: His Majesty's Stationary Office, 1942).

[18] Thomas Humphrey Marshall, *Citizenship and the Social Class* (Cambridge: Cambridge University Press, 1950).

[19] Henrik Christoffersen, *Det offentlige og samfundsudviklingen: træk af udviklingen efter 1945* (Copenhagen: Akademisk Forlag, 1978).

[20] Keynes as well as Beveridge and Marshall were liberals of political opinion. They envisioned a society in which the market and civil society were bearing organizational forms. The social reform, modeled on Beveridge's, in its original form did not contain any government funding contributions at all but was a compulsory insurance scheme with equal contributions for all. This, on the other hand, meant that it was the least well-off who determined the size of the benefits, and they had to be low by nature. But they also kept the least well-off from having to depend on the state. This side of the welfare state did not get adapted by Denmark. Here, it was probably important that the political system in Denmark was completely different from the British.

The Constitutional Change and the Emergence of Redistribution as the Raison D'Être of the State

When Denmark got the first constitution in 1849, the constitution was arranged with a two-chamber system. The government was Rigsdagen (from old Danish tradition where king who called a day of the realm to discuss policy) which consisted of a Folketing (House of Commons) and a Landsting (House of Lords). For the Folketing, there was equal and ordinary suffrage (for men of considerable age and of proper character). To the Landsting, only the property owners had the right to vote, and the King appointed members. All legislation had to be passed by both chambers. It was a compromise at the fall of the autocracy, where democracy was probably introduced, but where the property owners actually had a veto right over legislation, including redistribution. With the constitutional amendment in 1915, the Landsting passed to ordinary suffrage, and from the 1930s, identical political majorities were formed in both the Folketing and the Landsting. This triggered a constitutional amendment with the abolition of the Landsting, which was passed in 1953.

With the absolute equal and universal suffrage, it was definitively settled that a political majority could implement any redistributive legislation that they would want.[21] In economic theory, it is a trivial result that when the median voter has an income that is lower than the average income in society (which will always be the case in a free society), then half of the voters with the lowest incomes, if they are economically rational, form a voting coalition and vote for full redistribution. These voters will all have a smaller income than the average income and thus win by a redistribution that makes all incomes equal. Only rising costs of rising redistribution moderate this result on the assumption that everyone is governed solely by economic self-interest.

The constitutional amendment was made in light of the post-war period. Here, there was a strong notion that the horrors and victims of war must not have been in vain, but must lead to a better society in a better world. The time was marked by an intense debate on democracy, and it was a dominant view that conversation had to form the core of a modern and enlightened democracy. Particularly the prominent Social

[21] Henrik Christoffersen, *Det mindst ringe: Om demokratiet i velfærdsstaten* (Copenhagen: Multivers, 2014).

Democratic politician, theologian, and educator, Hal Koch, argued in the book 'What is Democracy' from 1945[22] for the notion that democracy is conversation—ideas, akin to those later suggested by Habermas.[23] Voting and "majority tyranny" were evil and should be avoided. Because of the general political agreement on these ideals, the 1953 constitution contained few if any checks and balances on majority rule. A potential issue, as the moral argument for democracy is not to give the majority what they want, but rather that the minorities are protected.[24]

On such an idealistic basis, Danish democracy was fundamentally changed so that it in principle opened up for a strong economic redistribution in society, although hardly anyone in the early 1950s imagined that such a strong redistribution would also be realized. In fact, however, it turned out that behind the discourse on conversational democracy, growth in the size of the public sector was gaining momentum. In practice, majority tyranny proved difficult to limit over time, as the constitution is based on ideals rather than rules for limiting majority power. Since there is also no real threefold division of power in the Danish constitution, it is straightforward for populist and opportunistic rulers to commit digressions against the Kochian understanding of democracy.[25]

[22] Hal Koch, *Hvad er demokrati?* (Copenhagen: Gyldendal, 1991).

[23] Rainer Forst, "The Discourse Theory of Morality: 'Discourse Ethics - Notes on a Program of Philosophical Justification' (1983)", In: *The Habermas Handbook* (New York Chichester, West Sussex: Columbia University Press, 2018), pp. 383–393.

[24] As issues with immigration came to the forefront in the twenty-first century, this issue became especially hot.

[25] Three examples spring to mind. The impeachment case against former Minister of Justice Erik Ninn-Hansen (1922–2014) who in the Tamil Case was charged with breaking the law to limit immigration rights. A current impeachment case is going against the former Minister for Immigration, Integration and Housing Inger Støjberg (b. 1973), who is also charged with potential law breaking to limit immigration. The current Prime Minister Mette Frederiksen (b. 1977) is likewise being investigated (at time of writing) if she broke the constitution when forcibly exterminating and outlawing the commercial breeding of mink doing COVID-19.

The Failed State and the Welfare State

Another way to view the creation of the welfare state in Denmark is through the failed state theory.[26] According to failed state theories, state survival is contingent on efficiency and legitimacy. In the case of Denmark, the state had, in various ways and with changing people in power, managed to modernize and create efficiency resulting in improved economic performance since the Danish State Bankruptcy of 1813. Legitimacy was independence, particularly from German rule, and while business and export was in large part focused on Britain and the world at large, civil servants and politicians on Slotsholmen (the house of government) was almost exclusively focused on the neighbor to the south. The promise was clear; society would prosper, and government guarantee that the country remained independent and free to trade.

With the German occupation of 1940, and particular the breakdown of the appeasement policy in 1943, the Danish state lost both legitimacy and efficiency and became a failed state if we follow the theory. Rule of law broke down and authority became arbitrary, while protest and sabotage grew. The whole role of business was disputed, particularly who you could trade with and who not not. Germany had won, and the state had done close to nothing to stop it.

After the war, the place of Denmark in the new world order was far from given. While most longed to belong to the allied side, several factors leaned in favor of what would later become the Warsaw pact. While Denmark had had a Resistance Movement, the majority of society for the majority of the war had followed appeasement, and the net effect of Danish policy and citizens had likely been positive for the Germans

[26] Fund for Peace failed state index—https://fragilestatesindex.org/; Christopher J. Coyne, "Reconstructing Weak and Failed States: Foreign Intervention and the Nirvana Fallacy", *Foreign Policy Analysis*, no. 2 (2006), pp. 343–361; Charles T. Call, "Beyond the 'Failed State': Toward Conceptual Alternatives", *European Journal of International Relations*, 17:2 (2010), pp. 303–326; Daron Acemoglu & James Robinson, *Why Nations Fail? The Origins of Power, Prosperity and Poverty* (London: Profile, 2012); Andrew Taylor, *State Failure* (London: Palgrave Macmillan UK, 2013); Robert H. Bates, "State Failure", *Annual Review of Political Science*, 11:1 (2008), pp. 1–12; Stewart Patrick, "'Failed' States and Global Security: Empirical Questions and Policy Dilemmas", *International Studies Review*, 9:4 (2007), pp. 644–662; Olivier Nay, "Fragile and Failed States: Critical Perspectives on Conceptual Hybrids", *International Political Science Review*, 34:3 (2013), pp. 326–341.

for most of the war effort.[27] As a result, the Soviet side held on to the island of Bornholm for a year after the German occupation. A year marked by violence and rape for the locals.[28] Danish politicians and civil servants could do little to help, while all spoke German almost none spoke English.[29] The popularity of communism also grew and the Communist party won their largest electoral victory with 12.5% of the votes in 1945.[30] What likely saved Denmark from the red menace was the historical happenstance that Greenland was part of the Danish Commonwealth and proved the needed bargaining chip for US support.[31]

Emerging as part of the Western world opened up for business, but the state was still de facto failed. However, the organization of the state apparatus, with the exception of the police and armed forces, had emerged basically undamaged. Public choice economics will tell us that the self-interest of public officials and elected politicians often matter more than the common good for policy outcomes, and this book argues that the members of the state organization was in search of a new survival strategy at this time. This is the true precursor to the redistributive state. It appears to many today, as a mystical time period lending itself to the narrative of a planned, natural, morally just, and rightful welfare state. This narrative is often attributed to Prime Minister Jens Otto Krag (1914–1978) who with the program "Denmark in the Future"[32] traced the welfare state

[27] Steen Andersen, *De gjorde Danmark større: de multinationale danske entreprenørfirmaer i krise og krig 1919–1947* (Copenhagen: Lindhardt og Ringhof, 2005); Steen Andersen, *Danmark i det tyske storrum: dansk økonomisk tilpasning til Tysklands nyordning af Europa 1940–41*. 2. ed. (Copenhagen: Lindhardt og Ringhof, 2004); Steen Andersen, "Mild Occupation? Denmark, 1940–1945", In: *Paying for Hitler's War: The Consequences of Nazi Hegemony for Europe* (New York: Cambridge University Press, 2016); Steen Andersen,*"Der er intet foruroligende for Danmark": Danmark mellem stormagterne frem mod den 9. april 1940* (Odense: Syddansk Universitetsforlag, 2020).

[28] Bent Jensen, *Den lange befrielse: Bornholm besat og befriet 1945–1946* (Odense: Odense Universitetsforlag, 1999).

[29] Søren Mørch, *25 statsministre: 25 fortællinger om magten i Danmark i det tyvende århundrede* (Copenhagen: Gyldendal, 2007).

[30] Paul Hammerich, *Fred og nye farer* (Copenhagen: Gyldendal, 1976).

[31] It is beyond the scope of this book to comment further on Danish cold war policy, but it remained shaky and divided throughout. The Left particularly had divided sympathies in the period.

[32] Socialdemokratisk Forbund, *Fremtidens Danmark* (Copenhagen: Fremad, 1945).

back to the even earlier program "Denmark for the People Program"[33] and painted the development of a universal welfare state as a narrative of planned, scientific, and the unavoidable next and potentially final step in Danish history.[34]

The real story is bleaker. Bearing a part of the responsibility of the appeasement policy choice, the Social Democrats faced competition from the communists. As a response, Social Democrats and Venstre—who wanted to further help agriculture interests—formed the "common people" alliance with an established and welcoming state apparatus embracing the redistributive state as new raison d'être.[35] The Danish state organization survived by creating the legitimacy from welfare, and providing efficiency in redistribution.[36] This was, to say the least, a mixed blessing for the business community. On the one hand, the compromised acknowledge wealth creation as fundamental for redistribution (and kept communism at bay), but on the other, the purpose of business became to share out the spoils.[37] It further mattered in cementing the welfare state debate in a narrative and mystical creation myth from which later historical facts are often judged.

The Final Breakthrough: The National Pension

With the emergence of a clearer redistributive policy aim, one could immediately expect a more confrontational political climate in the Folketing, where the parties against more redistribution and greater burdens placed on the well-to-do part of the electorate would try to revolt against the parties behind the majority. However, political rationality came to pull in a different direction. Now that only a political minority had the interest of averting more economic redistribution, it

[33] Socialdemokraterne, *Danmark for Folket: For Arbejde, Brød Og Frihed* (1934).

[34] Asmussen, "Danmark i kapitalismens guldalder: forholdet mellem den økonomiske politik og den samfundsøkonomiske udvikling i Danmark i 1950'erne". Hans Kryger Larsen, *Dansk industri efter 1870: Industri, stat og samfund 1939–1972*, Vol. 8 (Odense: Syddansk Universitetsforlag, 2008).

[35] Kjeld Bjerke, "Økonomiske Efterkrigstidsproblemer. Betænkning afgivet af Finansministeriets Udvalg af 30. Januar 1943", *Erhvervøkonomisk tidsskrift*, no. 9 (1945).

[36] Carsten Due-Nielsen, "Paul Hammerich: En danmarkskrønike 1945–72: Velfærd på afbetaling", *Historisk Tidsskrift*, 85:1 (1985).

[37] Hansen, "Økonomisk vækst i Danmark: 1720–1914".

would in any case be useless to offer simple resistance by refusing to vote for the majority redistribution policy. More constructive for a bourgeois policy against redistribution would be to enter into negotiations aimed at gaining influence and moderation. It turned out that most of the Folketing's legislation on welfare policy and tax policy was passed by broad political agreements, which spanned the middle of Danish politics. Keynesianism became deeply rooted into even parties of the right—once again proving the allure of the Keynesian message to vote-seeking politicians. This was the case under both Social Democratic and right-wing governments. Such a pragmatic dialogue-oriented policy also created a high degree of continuity in Danish politics, although also a not insignificant inertia.

When the National Pension Reform was adopted in 1956, it marked the real breakthrough of modern pragmatic welfare policy.[38] By desire of the right wing in parliament, all citizens were entitled to a national pension financed by a uniform tax on income. Part of the argument was that even AP Møller (1876–1965)—the rich man's stereotype of the time—should have a national pension, as later Prime Minister Viggo Kampmann expressed.[39]

The financing was arranged by a dedicated tax payment called "national pension contribution"—an additional flat rate of 2 tax points. This emphasized the nature of the scheme, which is basically an insurance scheme. The proceeds from the tax were also posted to a separate account in the state accounting department.[40]

When the national pension was created in 1956, it depended in a sense to a large extent on Venstre, although it was the Social Democrats, who at the time were the governing party. Venstre had originally been against a state public pension model as desired by the Social Democrats, but as agriculture had entered an ever deeper economic crisis after the late 1940s, the Venstre oriented itself toward welfare benefits, which

[38] Peter Baldwin, *The Politics of Social Solidarity—Class Bases of the European Welfare State, 1875–1975* (Cambridge: Cambridge University Press, 1990).

[39] Christoffersen, *Det mindst ringe: Om demokratiet i velfærdsstaten*; Smidt, *Viggo Kampmann: modig modstandsmand, klog finansminister, ustyrlig statsminister.*

[40] Due-Nielsen, "Paul Hammerich: En danmarkskrønike 1945–72: Velfærd på afbetaling".

also benefited the independent farmers.[41] Conservatives, on the other hand, maintained opposition to a definitive state takeover of responsibility for old-age support. The party spoke instead of models where personal responsibility was maintained, and in the following years, this line was translated into both the ATP organization and the start of building a labor market-based pension system (see Chapters 6 and 7). All this happened against the background of a state apparatus that had de facto failed and lost its legitimacy during World War II, and now was struggling to acquire new legitimacy and identity.

The Good Times That Changed Everything

Danish economy was characterized by weak and changing economic conditions from the end of the 1940s until around 1958. Thereafter, a sharp upswing set in. However, the Danish economy and economic policy were not geared to the new demand pressure, so the balance of payments quickly became negative, and inflation increased at the same time as unemployment completely disappeared. During the collective bargaining negotiations in 1961, demand pressure really took hold in very high wage increases. There was talk of a "wage celebration". It was not sustainable as wages rose faster than productivity, which put burdens on productivity and weakened exports.

The situation thus called for new mechanisms that could bring about a tolerable degree of socio-economic sustainability. Already during the period of stagnation in the mid-1950s, it had been realized that Denmark was lagging behind in establishing an effective coherent economic policy. Fiscal policy was eased too quickly by the incumbent government for the sake of employment as soon as the slightest opportunity in the form of foreign exchange earnings emerged, and it was tightened up too late due to the political costs thereby. As a consequence, Danmarks Nationalbank then tightened monetary policy instead, and this hurt investment and jobs in the long run. This situation gave rise to the Folketing setting up a committee with the task of finding ways to better coordinate economic policy. The Coordination Committee's report outlined a new body for carrying out the coordination task

[41] Baldwin, *The Politics of Social Solidarity—Class Bases of the European Welfare State, 1875–1975.*

based on a belief in common solutions for the benefit of all.[42] The report, which is supported by both the trade union movement and from the employer side, states that "from a long-term perspective, there can be no significant conflict of interest between employees, employers and the rest of society. For all parties, it is crucial how productivity develops". It expressed a Pareto economic growth argument that if the cake gets bigger, then there can be one more bite for everyone. The notions of economic equality that have become dominant in the later part of the history of the welfare state were completely absent here.

The proposal for an economic council rose up in the Danish Parliament in the light of the new economic boom, and the result was the creation in 1961 of the Economic Council. The rationale was that the country's strongest economists as a presidency should present the sharpest possible analysis of the Danish economic situation, and a council with representatives of authorities and interest groups must on that basis through consultation seek an agreement on a sustainable economic policy and on wage determination on the labor market.

The Economic Council never got to play the coordinating role it was ideally intended. The council's limitations became clear when they initially had ambitions to influence wage formation on the labor market. The labor-side immediately rejected an income policy and subordination to the council instructions. If income policy were to come into play, it would have to demand a completely different price, and here the workers' side set the demand for so-called economic democracy. The national federation of trade unions (LO) presented a model in which funds were to be built on an ongoing basis, which should gradually take over the ownership of the business enterprises, and which was managed centrally.

The struggle for economic democracy lasted from the early 1960s to the end of the following decade.[43] At no time was any reform of economic democracy carried out, but the struggle came to significantly block an effective balancing of economic policy. This is because the Social Democrats and trade unions met much resistance from both right and left, each worked with other reform proposals, and each had basic but different ideological misgivings about the proposal. In practice, all these

[42] Niels Kærgård, "Økonomiske vismænd - politiserende økonomer eller objektive eksperter", *Nationaløkonomisk Tidsskrift*, no. 134 (1996), pp. 113–127.

[43] Bent Rold Andersen, *Lønmodtagernes medejendomsret: rapport fra udvalget om lønmodtagernes medejendomsret* (Copenhagen: Det Kongelige Bibliotek, 1978).

reform ideas often came into play in most economic negotiations, and this made broader political cooperation on even minor issues difficult. The 1960s and 1970s were marked by decades of balance of payments deficits, government deficits, inflation, and high interest rates. After the oil crisis in 1973, there was also unemployment and weak and fluctuating economic growth in what economists described as stagflation.

In the first period of the Economic Council, it contributed strongly to the development of an explicit understanding of the welfare state economic rationale. The council's thinking was not least inspired by Swedish economists linked to the Swedish Social Democrats.[44] The economy was seen here as a dual system with a private exporting and foreign competing production sector and a domestic welfare sector. Here, economic stability will demand that the foreign competing sector be kept competitive and efficient so that it can finance welfare. This in turn demands that the welfare sector not become wage-leading and absorb labor force from the private sector, so that the private wage level is pushed up further. That feedback loop would result in inflation and loss of competitiveness. The competitiveness of the foreign competing sector must also be ensured by maintaining the sector on strict market economy terms.

However, it turned out in the early 1960s that the political and administrative system did not possess at all the ability or tools to control the development of the welfare sector under the new, strong demand pressure.[45] In contrast, the welfare sector entered a high-growth phase that lasted until the early 1980s.

The Ungovernable Welfare Sector

The most basic structures in the organization and economic governance of the welfare state in the first post-war period had been formed in the 1930s, when Social Democratic-led governments had for the first time

[44] Henrik Christoffersen, *Danmarks økonomiske historie efter 1960* (Herning: Systime, 1999); Gösta Edgren, Karl-Oluf Faxén, & Claes-Erik Odhner, *Lönebildning och samhällsekonomi* (Stockholm: Rabén & Sjögren, 1970).

[45] Bente Hansen (ed.), *Dengang i 60'erne: billeder fra dengang, tekster fra i dag* (Copenhagen: Information, 1979).

been given the opportunity to consolidate.[46] These structures, which had thus been designed at a time of low growth, unemployment, and downward pressure on prices and wages, remained largely unchanged until the beginning of the high-growth period after the end of the 1950s. The public expenditure side functioned with a financing system in which the approximately 1300 municipalities, many of which were quite small, accounted for a large part of the decision-making competence in the welfare sector. At the same time, the state had committed itself without reimbursement to a large part of the municipalities' expenses, whereby the municipalities really only had to make a very limited financial sacrifice to expand their welfare activities. The public revenue side functioned with a tax system where last year's tax paid could be deducted in the calculation of taxable income, and where interest paid also could be deducted in full.

The new situation at the beginning of the 1960s caused the public management and organization to produce quite different results than in the period before.[47] The municipalities now had the financial strength to take advantage of the strong financial incentive in the state reimbursement schemes for a sharp increase in activity. The state and government failed to balance the expansive effects of the economy with a tighter fiscal policy. On the one hand, the tax deduction right limited the possibility of taxation, and on the other hand, the interest deduction right became very expansive in relation to households, which set off an explosion in loan-financed detached house construction. This development was further fuelled by made possible by a liberalization of monetary and credit conditions from thier wartime restrictions.[48]

The economics professor Jørgen S. Dich had already in 1958 clearly exposed the welfare state as a completely uncontrolled system, although the modern Keynesian spirit of the time insisted that everything was manageable and under control. In Nationaløkonomisk Tidsskrift, he pointed out that the public welfare activities have not originated from

[46] Henrik Christoffersen, *Det offentlige og samfundsudviklingen: træk af udviklingen efter 1945.*

[47] Henrik Christoffersen, "Den udvidede forvaltning", In: Peter Bogason (ed.), *Stat, forvaltning og samfund efter 1950* (Copenhagen: Jurist og Økonomforbundets Forlag, 2000).

[48] Due-Nielsen, "Paul Hammerich: En danmarkskrønike 1945–72: Velfærd på afbetaling".

any general theory that a better system should be achieved for society as a whole. Dich believed that these activities arose from political demands made by different sections of the population with the intention of thereby achieving special benefits.[49]

Dich's analysis was further supported by the developments over the following years. Initially, the political response to strong demand pressures and to the tendencies toward inflation and deficits in the balance of payments and public finances was quite short-sighted. Political interventions were designed in 1962 and 1963 with a view to immediately ease the pressure, strongest with the "comprehensive solution" in 1963 with direct intervention to regulate prices and wages. However, the effect was only sporadic and quickly disappeared. It also began to demand a political understanding that more structural reforms were needed, but it was part of this understanding that such basic structural reforms required a completely new way of thinking and had to be thoroughly prepared so some time had to be set aside. However, political inertia was also pronounced. A withholding tax reform was implemented in 1969, but the unlimited interest deduction right was not moderated until 1987. A local government reform was implemented in 1970, but the conversion of local government funding into block grants and the design of a new division of tasks in the public sector was not completed until the end of the 1970s.

Along the way, a political powerlessness became apparent. In the mid-1960s, Social Democrat-led governments tried on several occasions to find reductions in public growth, but it did not prove politically possible to really rally around results in the so-called "vacuum cleaner gangs", an expression meant to describe the cleaning of undue costs. The center-right majority government, the VKR government from 1967 to 1971, declared an explicit goal to stop public growth: "Money is best when in the pockets of the citizens" became the conservative finance minister, Poul Møller (1919–1997), slogan. Nevertheless, the public growth rate set a record in these years.

Voters reacted strongly in the so-called "landslide election" of 1973, where a large part of the members of the Folketing were rejected, and

[49] Jørgen S. Dich, "Bidrag til belysning af den moderne velfærdsstats økonomiske problemer", *Nationaløkonomisk Tidsskrift*, no. 96 (1958).

where at that time, libertarian Fremskidtspartiet (Progress party)[50] and the populist Center Democrats entered the Folketing with a large number of seats. But the damage was difficult to repair, and for example the Social Reform from 1973, which was prepared during the 1960s boom, came to strain the country's economy ever since. It was state-initiated, and imposed heavy consumption requirements on the municipalities.

At the same time, there were other signs that strong public welfare growth was problematic. Jørgen S. Dich got an almost popular breakthrough with the book "The ruling class" in 1973,[51] when he in a popular way analyzed the public servants special opportunity to protect their own interests by boosting a welfare sector based on their dubious arguments. His designation of this advocacy and de facto a social exploitation of the rest of the population, caused a stir without, however, having a lasting influence.

The Too Late and Too Incomplete Reforms

It would require the development of completely new ideas about the organization and governance of the welfare state before Danish politics was ready to implement more fundamental structural reforms. The Ministry of Finance came to play the main role in this development. An extensive study was carried out here in the period around 1970, which led to the presentation of the so-called Perspective and Plan Review (persepktivplanredegørelsen, PP), PP1, and PP2 in 1971 and 1973.[52] In connection with the work, the first version of a Danish macroeconomic model, ADAM, was also developed.

[50] The party, and its legendary founder Mogens Glistrup (1926–2008), later changed to the first outspoken anti-immigrant party. It ultimately imploded in 1993, and from its ashes the Danish People Party was born: a party who quickly shed most remnants of libertarian economic policy for a Social-Democratic one and mainly focused on a populist platform of immigrant reform and benefits for the elderly. The party went from pariah status to forming the parliamentary foundations of most ruling government in the first two decades of the twenty-first century and grew to become the second largest party in parliament.

[51] Jørgen S. Dich, *Den herskende klasse* (Copenhagen: Borgen, 1973).

[52] Boligministeriet, *Perspektivplanlægning 1970–1985* (Copenhagen: Schultz Forlag, 1971); Finansministeriet, *PPII Perspektivplanredegørelse 1972 – 1985* (Copenhagen: Statens Trykningskontor, 1973).

It was a systematic development of an operational macroeconomic understanding that took place in those years. Likewise, it was absolutely essential that the thinking came to revolve around an understanding of the citizens as well as of municipalities and companies as rational and optimizing agents. The state's regulation was to be designed on the basis of insight into the economic incentives that the regulation entailed, rather than on the basis of legal and moral premises. With this, the ungovernability led to a strong consolidation of the state. The state was given or assumed the authority to relate to and attempt to control the agents' behavior at both the micro and macro levels.

In fact, the consolidation of the state took a form that was far from optimal from the point of view of economic efficiency. The municipalities came with the 1970s transition to be financed by block grants to be confronted with the full operating costs on the margin, but the multiplier of the balanced budget meant that in parallel, the municipal taxes increased and expenditures worked expansively at the macro level, so the municipalities continued to function with a strong incentive to expand their service sector. However, the municipalities had become so strong a political power factor that parliament had no success in attempting with the socio-economically efficient financing model. Consumption taxes in the form of turnover from 1962 and VAT from 1967 probably made consumers bear the main share of costs of increased consumption, however income taxes were not correspondingly eased, but instead increased due to the expansive dynamics of the welfare sector, which meant the taxes' total distortion losses went up. The benefit levels and duration periods of social policy were also increased, for example, because the recession of the oil crisis led to unemployment, as no agreement could be reached on a policy to strengthen competitiveness. Thus, the incentives for work were weakened. All in all, the state thus took a stronger grip on society and the economy, but did not achieve a stronger welfare economic efficiency from its governance.

The Dream of the Planned Welfare State

The basic idea behind the municipality reform around 1970 was that the planning of the rapidly growing urban communities of the time required stronger local authorities for the task, and that it was necessary to decentralize the management of the rapidly expanding local welfare production. There was also a need for a stronger link so the hospital system could be decentralized from the state on the one hand and taken by the other hand from the municipalities to regional authorities. In this new organizational system, it was not only necessary to renew the financing arrangements but also to develop completely new ways of ensuring coherence. To this end, work was initiated in the late 1960s to develop an all-encompassing system of economic planning, which was also quite in the spirit of the times, along with student uprisings and Marxism gaining intellectual traction.[53] The completed but never fully realized planning system was described in a report from the Ministry of Finance in 1975.[54] The system was designed as a large plan matrix with cross-cutting plans for business development, distribution, physical structures and finances, respectively, as well as with sector plans in municipalities and regions in all significant public task areas and referring to the planning centers in the central administration for each of the cross-cutting plan areas. At the top to coordinate all economic planning, a Government Planning Committee was to be established with all the central ministers.

Throughout the mid-1970s, great efforts were made to get such a system to work, but at no time was it possible to make it truly operational. The municipalities moved the coming year's activity plan upward year by year, and the multi-year part of the plans merely legitimized the current imbalance by describing the creation of balance in the following years. In addition, the plans were strongly focused on how much more of the already familiar would be delivered in the future, while innovation and productivity advances were completely excluded from the planning. The system came to stand as a monument to the romantic and dreamlike socialism of the 1970s, and it died out after the change of government in 1982.

The Wall

The share of public expenditure in the national product grew continuously throughout the period up to the early 1980s, but then this growth stopped. This can be immediately understood in the light of the dramatic

[53] Hansen, *Dengang i 60'erne: billeder fra dengang, tekster fra i dag*.

[54] Udvalget vedrørende centraladministrationens planlægningsvirksomhed, *Betænkning nr. 743* (1975).

imbalance that had developed in the Danish economy.[55] It is noteworthy that the slowdown in 1982 proved to be definitive.

An obvious explanation for this rupture is that the welfare distortion losses in further public growth proved to be greater than acceptable. Quite possibly, an even larger public sector would also demand more fundamental societal changes with restricted freedom and democracy and with a stronger controlling state power. Potentially moving Denmark all the way to a socialist institutional logic rather than the social logic which was overtaking the liberal of yesteryears.

With this, the premises of politics in the welfare state were fundamentally changed. New expansive measures became in principle only possible if funding could be allocated by limiting other measures. The political process takes place around annual budget laws (Finansloven) and municipal budgets. In principle, this means that the elected politicians, after having done their utmost to make the best possible use of the resources present, must immediately start making decisions again about changes in the use of resources. This dilemma probably led to some political stagnation, but the logic of the political system, on the other hand, promised that politicians would constantly make decisions that could secure their voter support. Therefore, with the unchanged size of the public sector, financial resources must still be mobilized for new initiatives. Closing down public activities has only to a limited extent been politically possible, and that meant that freeing resources to the welfare state had to be provided by savings on existing activities.

This reality must be seen in connection to the fact that public welfare provision has already been up against the so-called Baumol effect,[56] which consists in the fact that a public wage development in parallel with the private sector will create increasing expenditure pressure due to productivity growth in the private sector but not in the public sector.

All in all, it has thus characterized the welfare state since the early 1980s that it has been under constant pressure to procure resources within the largely familiar field of activities so that the welfare state's politicians can constantly buy voters. It can be seen positively as still productivity growth, but at least the 800,000 public employees and their

[55] Christoffersen, *Danmarks økonomiske historie efter 1960.*

[56] Willam J. Baumol, *The Cost Disease* (New Haven, Yale University Press, 2012); Christoffersen, *Det mindst ringe: Om demokratiet i velfærdsstaten.*

organizations and users of welfare have probably rather been oriented in the direction of talking about cuts. One could also raise the question of why the politicians of the welfare state only implemented savings so late, if it could be done without reduced dividends. The optimistic beliefs of the early post-war period in the good welfare state have at least been greatly modified. At the same time, the concept of welfare has expanded. More and more often people talk about schools, museums, and even the national broadcasting corporation (DR) as being welfare, on the other hand, the majority of Danes today have a hard time understanding that tax breaks can be welfare, which they typically are in economic theory—as illustrated in the debate after the Liberal Alliance party had the slogan: "Tax cuts are also welfare".

Incidentally, the new premise of linking new welfare to savings on existing welfare tended to make welfare policy look like a zero-sum game. If anyone should have more, then there were others who had to give something up. The political rhetoric came to reflect this. The distribution debate came to revolve around the new concept of inequality. This ensures that it will appear as morally problematic to create wealth through one's own efforts, but more righteous to increase prosperity through the state and political decisions.

New Public Management: The Introduction of Misunderstood Business Thinking

The collapse of the ambitions to develop the welfare state to be a truly planned society with collective fund ownership of the means of production called for a new rationale for organization and management in the welfare society. Again, it would be Britain that was the inspiration, but this time for a new right-wing coalition government which were strongly market-oriented. The emphasis was on learning from business management and about letting competition and market forces play a bigger role. Bureaucracy, on the other hand, came to be seen as something negative. A small number of state-owned companies were sold,[57] but otherwise the vision of competition and market incentives was really only modestly implemented. An experiment with free municipalities only ever

[57] Henrik Christoffersen & Martin Paldam, "Privatization in Denmark 1980–2002", In: Marko Köthenbörger, Hens-Werner Sinn & John Whalley (ed.), *Privatization Experiences in the European Union* (Boston: MIT Press, 2010).

touched on trifles. Outsourcing progressed very slowly due to municipal obstruction, and the same was true of the much debated free choice solutions meant to stimulate competition in public production.

On the other hand, under the heading New Public Management, a management system in the public sector was developed, tied up with requirements for the production of detailed data at all levels and far-reaching detailed regulation and control based on data. The vision of a more market-oriented model of society was thus reversed after the early 1980s, so that it ended up in a further bureaucratized and centrally controlled society. NPM became its own negation. This, incidentally, coincides with a historical growth in the number of office staff, academics, and middle managers in the public sector. The composition and background of the civil service have also changed enormously, possibly further promoted by changes in the conditions of employment and remuneration of the self-proclaimed servants of the community. The plain truth is that business effectiveness comes largely from market competition, and of that there was very little exposure for the welfare state production.

Reforms and Labor Supply

The lesson that the Social Democrats learned from the collapse of the Anker Jørgensen (1922–2016) government was not forgotten within the party. The desire for a more "socially responsible" society was the product the Social Democrats sold to their voters, but it was bought by the citizens in the post-war period in anticipation of economic responsibility and respect for democratic institutions. Anker Jørgensen had put the population's confidence in the Social Democrats fiscal responsibility to the test. When the party again took office after the fall of the Schlüter government in 1993, it was differently oriented in relation to pursuing solid economic policies. The party would not risk putting the stabilization of previous years out of control. So while probably the new Nyrup government wanted to stimulate the economy, it had to be done in a responsible way. This led the government to embark on a reform process in relation to the labor supply, which was to be continued through the following decades.[58] The Nyrup government's probably most remembered contribution to these reforms was a modification of the early retirement scheme (efterlønnen), which Nyrup had otherwise promised to preserve in the heat of the election campaign. It was to prove to be politically costly for this government, but nonetheless, reforms to increase the supply of labor were carried on even after the Nyrup government. With the economic management culture prevailing in the Ministry of Finance, it became clear to all political parties around the political center that the welfare state in its fairly well-known form could only be continued in an economically viable way if labor supply was increased with further reforms.

The reform strategy for increasing labor supply also took place in the 1980s, when a Schlüter government in 1983, following pressure from an odd alliance between industry and the socialist parties, carried out a large weakening of immigration policy, thus triggering an immigration of non-educated Muslim workers who were sought after for industrial jobs. The longer prospects were utterly repressed, and while the status of newcomers gradually changed from guest workers to immigrants, the technological development and the shift of primitive work tasks to low-wage countries made this labor pool unattractive. As these immigrants have proven difficult to integrate into Danish society and Danish culture, they have developed into a significant economic burden at the same time as ghetto problems and other social problems have emerged, largely due to a failed Social Democratic policy of council estates.[59] It therefore became clear that an increase in the labor supply had to be largely mobilized domestically, and possibly from Eastern Europe, which became an integral part of the European community in the years after 1989. Despite increasing efforts, not least driven by the rise of the Danish People's Party, society failed to solve the integration challenge and it would prove to be the main political theme of the first two decades of the twenty-first century.

[58] At the onset of the Nyrup government's active fiscal policy was pursued, something Venstre were keen to mention. Particularly, experiments with large-scale state-financed furlough schemes proved that Danes like to vacation on other Danes's kroner as the saying went. Needless to say, these schemes had a negative impact on labor supply and was removed, so the final legacy of Nyrup's tenure as Prime Minister provided an increase in total labor supply.

[59] Stefan K. Sløk-Madsen, David Skarbek, Andreas Hansen, & Alexander Rezaei, "The Organization of Danish Gangs: a Transaction Cost Approach", *Trends in Organized Crime*, 24:3 (2021), pp. 1–17.

Conclusion

At the end of the twentieth century, the Danish welfare model had resulted in outcomes and institutional arrangements where further growth in relation to the overall size of the public economy has become difficult, unless the social model must be changed in the direction of less freedom and greater state collectivization. The general firm-driven globalization and the emergence of fundamental cross-border as well as unavoidable collective challenges entail great challenges for the Danish welfare state too. The welfare state in the Danish form developed into an extremely redistributive individual consumer society under the guise that in its origins after 1945, it was a national and democratic matter, where citizenship and the rights of the citizens in the Marshallian sense were crucial. This made the welfare state a redistribution machine between the "members", where individual welfare goods functioned as "means of payment" in line with cash benefits and progressive taxes.

When absolutism was abolished in Denmark with the first constitution, a ministerial system was established to organize the civil service. In the first government, a Ministry of Finance, a Ministry of War, a Ministry of the Navy, a Ministry of Justice, a Ministry of Foreign Affairs, a Ministry of Culture, and a Ministry of Trade were formed. In other words, a system in a classical liberal spirit or within the liberal institutional logic, which largely only took care of the provision of strategic collective services and goods, later formed the framework for a free social life. Here, the state took care of the type of public goods where individual payment was not possible and where the use by one did not exclude the simultaneous use by others, whereby the market was not expected to be able to provide these goods. In the welfare state, these basic collective activities have come to play a rather modest role, at least in terms of economic resource consumption, where the provision of public goods today constitutes a very limited share compared to individual welfare goods and transfer incomes.[60] That is the real paradox of the welfare state. The liberal society focused on the strategic collective needs of society. The Danish welfare state is instead about individual consumption of private goods in the form of welfare services and transfers. The welfare state was

[60] Finansministeriet, *Økonomisk Analyse – udviklingen i de offentlige udgifter fra 2000–2017* (2018), https://www.ft.dk/samling/20171/almdel/FIU/bilag/116/1891908.pdf, Accessed Jan 25, 2022.

founded without many checks and balances in a more naïve time, but has developed to its natural conclusion as a struggle of special interests in the name of democracy. The democratic coherence argument goes that the tax-paying earning minority also gets a sense of community when democracy forces it to pay the services and transfer services to the majority. An argument that is almost formulated as a threat in a time of rising populism and tribalist *realpolitik*.

Finally, there is a discourse within Danish welfare debates that somehow the original welfare ideal became corrupted, from noble beginnings to a perverted technocracy.[61] Such arguments do not stand scrutiny. The welfare state has similar intentions—good and bad—now as it has always had, and it has similar mechanism providing rent-seeking for well-organized special interest groups that manage to appeal to voters' sympathy—often at the expense of the more truly needy. An off shoot of the "mythical welfare state" debate is that some people wonder why this original welfare state ideal was abandoned with the reform agenda from the Schlüter government onward. This is not a very interesting question. The answer is simple economic necessity. The more interesting question is why Keynesian policies become so prevailing politically to the point that institutional logics fundamentally changed.[62] This should be a key point of wonder, as Denmark had been very successful as a liberal country from 1870 to 1920, but ended the twentieth century as a social one with a whole host of problems to boot and finance.

[61] Examples from general debate of this idea are plentiful. For more academic propositions, see Pedersen, *Konkurrencestaten*; Anders Lundkvist, *Dansk kapitalisme: gennembrud, storhed og stagnation* (Gjern: Hovedland, 2017).

[62] Asmussen, "Danmark i kapitalismens guldalder: forholdet mellem den økonomiske politik og den samfundsøkonomiske udvikling i Danmark i 1950'erne".

CHAPTER 4

Competing Explanations for Danish Prosperity

Much history deals with myth. Myths are narratives adapted by people to explain the context of lives and constraints on choices both personally and on a policy-level, as grounded in some past historical circumstances, the details of which matter little.[1] The general adherence to the universal welfare state is so little questioned today in Denmark across the spectrum of voters, making Nelson suggests that the welfare state is a modern secularized religion and continuation of Lutheranism.[2] While the precise reasons behind the creation of the welfare state are mythical to many, it was not planned and whatever the intentions the consequence speak a dire language as discussed in Chapter 3. In this chapter, I will further investigate some overarching narratives encountered when explaining why the prosperity level and institutional arrangement of Denmark is as observed. Some of these are closer to general myths, while others are established theories.

There certainly are grounds for wonder. The large growth period was not primarily in the twentieth century but from roughly 1830–1920,

[1] Jordan B. Peterson, *12 Rules for Life: An Antidote to Chaos* (London: Penguin UK, 2018).

[2] Robert H. Nelson, *Lutheranism and the Nordic Spirit of Social Democracy: A Different Protestant Ethic* (Aarhus: Aarhus Universitetsforlag, 2017).

© The Author(s), under exclusive license to Springer Nature Switzerland AG 2022

S. K. Sløk-Madsen, *Danish Capitalism in the 20th Century*, Palgrave Studies in Economic History,
https://doi.org/10.1007/978-3-031-04267-6_4

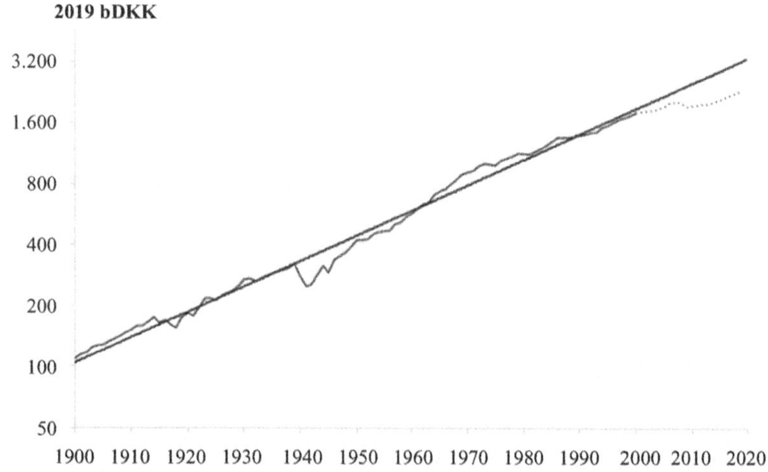

Fig. 4.1 GDP growth trend in fixed prices 1900–2020 (*Notes* Logarithmic scale. Statistic Denmark data for 1966–2019. Prior data from Maddison Project is utilized. *Source* Statistics Denmark, Maiddison Project. Cepos)

while we see declining growth with the introduction of the welfare state. The average growth of the twentieth century was roughly 3%, the average growth from 1986 to 2018 was however only 1.6, with 0.5 coming from modern reforms.[3] Growth has increased the living standard of the average Dane between 500 and 700% since 1900,[4] particularly the lowest 40% have had the relatively largest improvement, with around 10% coming from redistribution and 90% from economic growth.[5] With such numbers, it seems clear that explanations of Danish Prosperity is interesting both historically, but also for current policy (Fig. 4.1).

[3] Thomas Due Bostrup & Otto Brøns-Petersen, "Hvordan hæver vi væksten til 3 pct.?", *CEPOS* (2021), https://CEPOS.dk/artikler/hvordan-haever-vi-vaeksten-til-3-pct/, Accessed Jan 25, 2022.

[4] Ibid.

[5] Otto Brøns-Petersen, "Uden økonomisk vækst ville lavindkomsternes vækst i levestandard gennem 100 år have været en tiendedel af den faktiske", *CEPOS* (2021), https://CEPOS.dk/media/5970/uden-oekonomisk-vaekst-ville-lavindkomsternes-vaekst-i-levestandard-gennem-100-aar-have-vaeret-mindre-end-en-tiendedel-af-den-faktiske.pdf, Accessed Jan 25, 2022.

The Consensus Explanation

The overarching explanation for Danish policy choices is an explanation of consensus. It is an explanation that manifests itself in several versions, but which generally can be described as Danish society consisting of a state producing welfare paid by redistribution from a market generating profit. Neither is viewed as more important nor should take precedence in the explanation, but is equally dependent on each other. In the explanation, each side is ideally represented by two equally powerful special interest groups and together they form a compromise which creates democratic coherence.[6]

Empirically the theory has several things going for it. The decisions that shaped the welfare state was indeed often political compromises over the middle of the political spectrum between groups who might ideally favor more extreme arrangements. It is also empirically confirmed in that Denmark is a mixed economy with on the one hand a very liberal open market, and on the other hand a large state with massive redistribution.

What is challenging for the explanation is the precise nature of the alternative to a policy of compromise? After the system change of 1901, there was no way Denmark could be realistically governed by a small upper class elite. On the other side, the only time Denmark was in any real danger of becoming a communist country was in 1946 and even at that time it would have required substantial help from the USSR. Further troubling for the explanation is the development of the welfare coalition where a majority of voters are dependent on redistribution for their wages as shown in Fig. 4.2. In other words, the redistribution is taken from an increasingly smaller minority as shown in Fig. 4.3. In that light, the explanation seems less like a consensus, and more like a tyranny of majority. A tendency pointed out already in 1973 by leftwing theorist Dich[7] and potentially made worse by the later professionalization of policy.[8] The consensus explanation can be viewed as a policy of "cruel necessity" and

[6] Nevers, *Det produktive samfund: seks kapitler af industrialiseringens idéhistorie*.

[7] Dich, *Den herskende klasse*.

[8] Voter turnout for Danish elections is still impressive (2019: 84.6%), but the social status of politicians is very low. The Kantor Gallup Group reported in spring 2019 that 74% believed politicians to be primarily motivated by reelection. The membership of parties likewise is at the lowest levels. The largest party, the Social Democrats, both in terms of voters (2018 election: 914,882—25.9%) and members boost a member base of 40,000, down from the historic high of 300,000. Politicians themselves seems very

is likely experienced as such by voters. It can also tell a positive story that Danish politicians and other influential stakeholders no matter their degree of extremism understand that ultimately the Danish state and the free market go hand in hand as in the picture on the Jelling Stone. Or it might simply be that modern Danish policy is a continued balancing act by politicians to secure votes without causing too much long-term damage in the process.

Public dependence, 1.000 persons, 1970 and 2021		
	1970	**2021**
Public employees (x)	359	833
Recipients of public support (y)	819	2.208
Public dependents (x+y = z)	1.178	3.041
Voting age populace (a)	3.571	4.692
Share of a that is z	33,0%	64,8%

Notes: Recipients are full year recipients and includes people in taxfunded employment programs.
There is no figure for such programs for 1970
- it is not likely to matter much as such programs are a more modern invention.
Source: Statistics Denmark. FIU answer to question 176 of Feb 13. 2013, Økonomisk Redegørelse. Cepos calculations.

Fig. 4.2 Electoral dependence on redistribution (*Notes* Recipients are full year recipients and includes people in tax-funded employment programs. There is no figure for such programs for 1970—it is not likely to matter much as such programs are a more modern invention. *Source* Statistics Denmark. FIU answer to question 176 of Feb 13. 2013, Økonomisk Redegørelse. Cepos calculations)

keen on slightly changing the game too, most recently passing a law to politically appoint ambassadors.

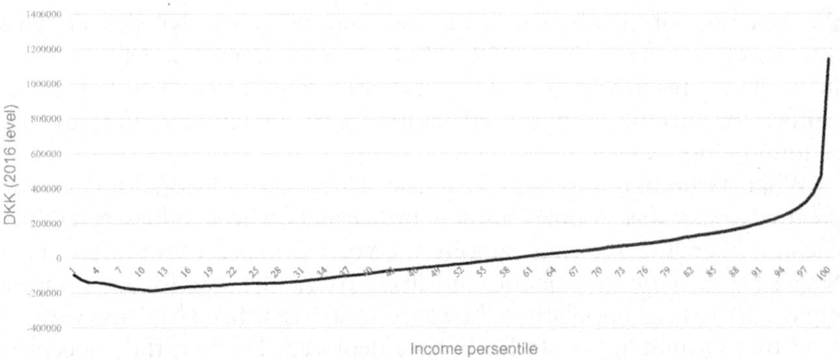

Fig. 4.3 Net contribution to public sector per income percentile, 2014 (*Source* Statistics Denmark)

The Common People Hypothesis

The defeat of 1864 made it clear that growth and wealth was to come from within the borders of Denmark, not from territorial aspirations. This internal focus was already part of the creed of Scandinavia as the region moved from centerstage to the periphery of the World and the past empires crumbled against forces whose might surpassed what even a theoretical unified Scandinavia at the time could hope to raise. In Denmark, the sentiment was most condensed expressed in a commemorative coin issued for the industrial fair in Copenhagen in 1872 and read in the words of the poet H.P. Holst (1811–1893): "So that all external loses shall be replaced, by what is lost externally, shall be won internally" (For hvert et tab igen erstatning findes; hvad udad tabtes, det må indad vindes). These words summed up the political ambition of the time and are often quoted to this day.[9]

Gone forever were the illusions of grandeur. Small became a virtue in itself. Small was manageable. Small was good. Investments continued and intensified in modernizing and industrializing the country side and that propelled it from a level of relative poverty to real richness.[10] Among the common people, the folk, a new vision also grew up around

[9] Kjeld Hansen, *Det tabte land* (Copenhagen: Gads Forlag, 2018).

[10] Thomsen, "Industri, stat og samfund, 1870–1939".

the teaching of theologian, educator, and politician Nikolaj Frederik Severin Grundtvig (1783–1872). While a controversial and lively figure in his time, his teaching had a substantial impact on Danish national culture, promoting common education, local community, and equality, as foundational values.[11]

While Grundtvignism was originally based on individualism, praised creativity, and was popular among the farmers whose values resembled classical liberalism the most among the voter groups, it also inspired the Social Democratic movement, and likely paved the way for its immense rapid and lasting popularity—however in a bastardized version without God that Grundtvig would likely have deplored. Further, the concept of farmers and the urban working class sharing a cultural heritage that could supersede divergent economic interests was laid.

Over time, the virtues of the small nation and equality creed developed into a virtue of mediocracy. The law of Jante came to rule. In terms of business, it was positively associated with flat hierarchies, meritocracy, as well as the open sharing of ideas. However, also negative cultural aspects followed for entrepreneurship, ambition, and even innovation are viewed with skepticism. It is economically sound in that it promotes work, but also dampens the economic focus as it has clear limits to the acceptance of material motivation being in its core a spiritual movement, which gave social leniency toward non-contributors.

All this creates the hypothesis or false narrative that Denmark is composed of one common people, a folk, that might disagree on the details, but are united on values and therefore compromising, after honest conflict, is in itself seen as a goal.[12] It can be argued that the common people hypotheses is the motivation for the consensus explanation theory. By relying on smallness, the will of the people will manifest in popularity and celebration, which give legitimacy to both the market and the state.[13] The beginnings might have been Grundtvig, but today it is just as associated with Jens Otto Krag.

[11] Dybdahl et al., *Danmarks historie: De nye klasser 1870–1913.*

[12] Lundkvist, *Dansk kapitalisme: gennembrud, storhed og stagnation.*

[13] Fellman et al., *Creating Nordic Capitalism: The Business History of a Competitive Periphery.*

The Lost Opportunity Paradigm

The common people hypothesis and the consensus explanation are the most accepted and heralded explanations for Danish prosperity and the institutional arrangements. However, it has recently come under renewed scrutiny from acclaimed historian Per Boje.[14] His argument goes that while it is most definitely true that Denmark prospered in the twentieth century, we could have prospered more had other policy choices been made. Boje's theory moves the focus from the consensus as the cause of prosperity and rather focus on the lasting institutions as they formed prior to the twentieth century. Indeed already at the beginning of the nineteenth century. He shows that already under absolutism was there a policy movement toward free markets to fund the state—long before any talk of popular movements or consensus can be argued to matter. He also highlights that Denmark was looking more than previously believed internationally for policy and commercial inspiration—and from an earlier period. This was however centered around a small elite spearheaded by the monarchy. This economic order suffered by the Danish participation in the Napoleonic Wars however, but was quickly—and well before the 1848 constitution—replaced by a new personally involved and highly skilled class of urban entrepreneurs.[15]

These institution, were meant to, and fairly effective in, promoting urban industry and innovation, particularly spearheaded by a privileged higher bourgeois. This is the polar opposite of both the Common People Hypothesis and the Consensus Explanation, where prosperity is created from a democratic bottom-up approach. Bojes argument is further that the victory of parliamentarism in 1901, and helped by the two bank scandals and the global bank crisis in the first three decades, hindered the innovative potential in the urban elites by dampening their political popularity. While the nation did become rich, this caused the nation to become not as rich as it could have become, had the urban elites had more influence. Particularly, as the main wealth creator for the small state was the international outlook common among the urban elites and innovistic firm-based capitalism, but missing in most of the countryside and among the working classes at the time.

[14] Boje, *Vejen til velstand - marked, stat og utopi: Om dansk kapitalismes mange former gennem 300 år.*

[15] Hansen, "Økonomisk vækst i Danmark: 1720–1914".

Boje's thesis further fits well with the important work by economist Deirdre McCloskey.[16] In her theory, she argues that the urban bourgeoisie utilized virtues that let to cooperation, industriousness and particularly innovation which helped propel prosperity forward. It is particularly interesting to align her work focused on innovation rather than capital accumulation, as the main wealth creator to the Boje theory of Danish prosperity, as the landholding farmers and their alliance partners in the social engineering Social Democrats, very much focused on capital, not innovation, in their policy. Particularly so after 1945. Boje's work show how the twentieth century, particularly the last half as not a success, but rather a lost opportunity for wealth creation from the change of dominant institutional logic.[17] In an almost unholy alliance, the farmers and Social Democrats met over their shared Gruntvigian roots and used the efficient state apparatus and the policy vacuum of post-1945 to bleed the profit of innovative firm-based capitalism for their own special interests.

Trust and Danish Capitalism

Trust is very important for markets. If there is little to no trust, transaction cost rises as opportunism becomes rampant.[18] With lower transaction cost there is more trade, and more surplus. It is easier for local companies to expand both nationally and internationally, and it is easier for foreign companies and investments to take hold, which in turn creates innovation and healthy competition.

Danes display large trust in each other, as well as in state institutions and officials. Corruption is low and institutional robustness high.[19] There is a clear empirical connection between the size of a welfare state and the

[16] Deirdre N. McCloskey, *The Bourgeois Virtues: Ethics for an Age of Commerce* (Chicago: University of Chicago Press, 2006); Deirdre N. McCloskey, *Bourgeois Dignity: Why Economics Can't Explain the Modern World* (Chicago: University of Chicago Press, 2011).

[17] See Chapter 3 for a detailed discussion. See also Smelser & Swedberg, *The Handbook of Economic Sociology*; O'Riain, "States and Markets in an Era of Globalization"; Thornton, Lounsbury, & Ocasio, *The Institutional Logics Perspective: A New Approach to Culture, Structure, and Process*.

[18] Oliver E. Williamson, "Opportunism and Its Critics", *Managerial and Decision Economics*, 14:2 (1993), pp. 97–107.

[19] Transparancy International Survey (2020).

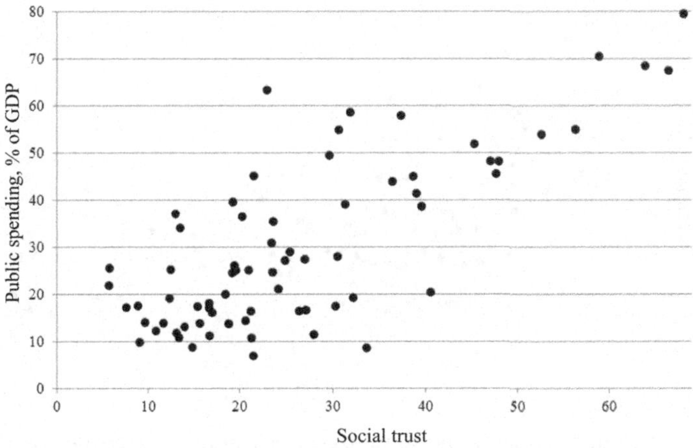

Fig. 4.4 Public spending and social trust correlation (*Source* Bjørnskov 2016)

level of social trust in society.[20] Traditional social conflict theory argues that if there are large inequalities in income or opportunities, that groups of people in society will have a harder time trusting each other as they have a harder time simply understanding others' point of view. Further, corruption is more favorable to the well-offs than the not so well-offs.[21] For instance on education access. But if the upper echelons of society are incorruptible, it will serve as a role model to society at large. All such theories state that the welfare state creates trust, can further trust with the right reforms, and destroy trust, with the wrong ones. There sure seem to be a large correlation between welfare state and trust, just like there is between inequality and trust, as Figs. 4.4 and 4.5 shows.

But as Bjørnskov points out, how does this approach to trust generation explain the great economic outputs before the welfare state? He and others argues the causality to be reversed. Rather than create social trust, welfare states rely on preexisting social trust to exist. Particularly as the social problems engaged by the welfare state and the resulting collective coercion would require a high level of trust ex-ante for voters to

[20] Christian Bjørnskov, "Tillid Og Velfærdsstaten", *Tidsskrift for Professionsstudier*, 12:22 (2016), pp. 22–28.

[21] Ibid.

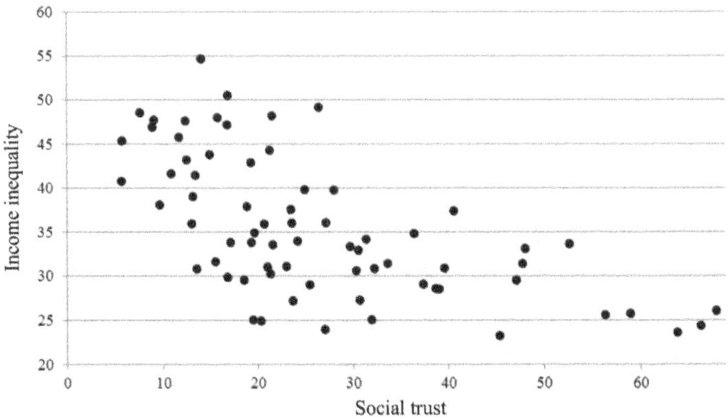

Fig. 4.5 Income inequality and social trust correlation (*Source* Bjørnskov 2016)

accept. People who trust each other are simply more likely to vote for redistribution.[22]

Bjørnskov's research further states three important preexisting trust fundamentals needed for the welfare state, but likely not promoted by it; (1) Citizens might worry about free riding when introducing redistributive policies, but less so if they are already trusting toward each other. (2) If the bureaucracy was not trustworthy it would be too costly to maintain, and finally (3) tax avoidance would be higher in a less trusting society, hence the revenue needed for a welfare state would be endangered.

Also, the long-term stability of institutions and society in Denmark also makes it more likely that trust levels predate the welfare state. Hence, trust holds significant explanatory power for Danish prosperity, but predates both the twentieth century and the welfare state. In financial cooperation trust likely also matters. When Danish banks jointly formed the company PBS (Nets) in 1968 to invest in shared electronic payment solution development, which included the 1983 launch of the Dankort—a national payment card—they were truly pioneers in developing the finan-

[22] Hans Pitlik & Ludek Kouba, "Does Social Distrust Always Lead to a Stronger Support for Government Intervention?" *Public Choice*, 163:3–4 (2015), pp. 355–377.

cial infrastructure in part responsible for the commercial success of the Internet—such cooperation among competitors also requires trust among the banks, internally in the banks, and from society.

The Role of a Homogeneous Population

Relating to both trust and the welfare state is the degree of homogeneity in the population. Two distinct and popular myths of homogeneity have grown from the Peoples Hypothesis. The first relates to homogeneity of policy. An idea that Danes have been largely in agreement on major policy issues since 1848 due in large part to the shared Grundtvigian virtues, and that main historical outcomes, like the welfare state, were planned. The Lost Opportunity Paradigm and the actual history (see Chapter 3) would place this as a myth. Further, one must question the validity of the shared Grundtvig heritage. While his figure and the original movement are a tangible fact, his precise philosophy is complex and often contractionary. In that he does resemble the actual society, but it is questionable to what degree a complex thinker that inspired such a diverse set of intellectual children to such different conclusions can be said to hallmark policy homogeneity. This is further backed up in value surveys, where Danes are not markedly more homogeneous than more multiethnic nations.[23]

A second, and some would say, more sinister myth of homogeneity, states that Danes are in agreement on major policy because they are financially and ethnically homogeneous. Or equal as the left would likely put it. Again, we should investigate the causality. Hayek famously theorized that as more decisions are taken by the state, the state will promote homogeneity and punish deviance.[24] Some data could suggest he was right. The top income inequality has fallen dramatically (see Fig. 4.6), and while income inequality has risen in the latest decades (see Fig. 4.7), all family types has been better off, expect those most heterogeneous (typically non-western immigrants with a strong preference for Islamic Values) and socially at risk youths as shown in Fig. 4.8. The policy choices of

[23] Christian Bjørnskov, "Hvor homogene er danskerne egentlig?", *Punditokraterne* (2014), https://punditokraterne.dk/2014/11/16/hvor-homogene-er-danskerne-egentlig/, Accessed Jan 25, 2022.

[24] Bruce Caldwell & F. A. Hayek, *The Road to Serfdom: Text and Documents: The Definitive Edition* (London: Taylor and Francis, 2014).

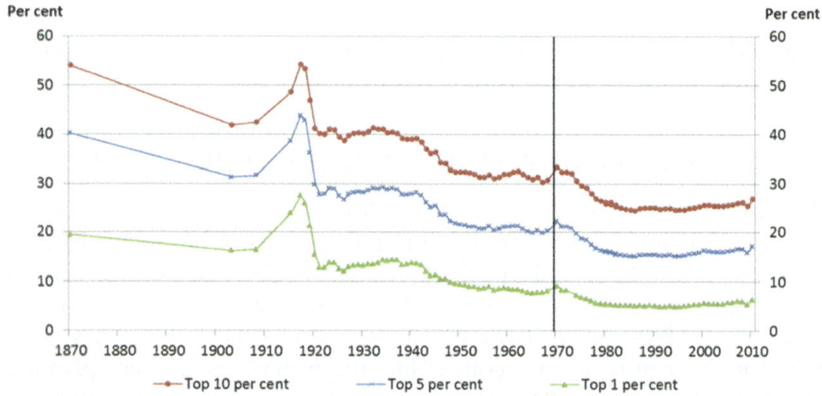

Fig. 4.6 Top income shares (*Notes* The vertical line in 1970 indicates the change from family to individual taxation. *Source* Atkinson, A.B. and Søgaard, J.E., 2016. The long-run history of income inequality in Denmark. *The Scandinavian Journal of Economics*, *118*(2), pp. 264–291)

the welfare state further promote homogeneity, for instance, with large control of how maternity and paternity leave is held. Further there are limits to tax rebates for families not wanting to use the state-financed daycare institutions and have both parents working (the norm), which de facto punishes families who wish to deviate from the norm.[25]

A lot of the immigration policy have been centered on the myth that homogeneity was a goal in itself, much to the dismay of the business sector. The policy norm toward the end of the twentieth century became, that immigrations problems came with immigrants, and should be solved by converting to the homogeneity standard. This is basically surrendering to a notion that public monopolies currently existing within areas such as education and health care is not only poorly suited to care for a growing diversity of preferences, but in fact is endangered by them.

Further, prosperity of a small developed nation needs foreign labor in both the top and low end of the skill pool and this is likely more important than homogeneity for prosperity. So, while a changing population

[25] Anne Kirstine Sørensen, *Moderland: når staten kupper børnene* (Copenhagen: Gad, 2020).

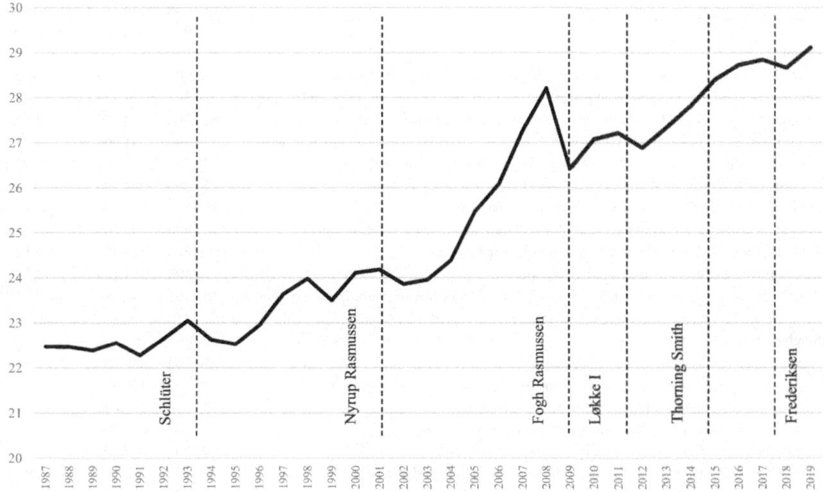

Fig. 4.7 Growth of Gini-coefficient under all modern Prime Ministers (*Source* Cepos, Statistics Denmark, Own Calculation)

comes with new challenges, it is more likely a new cost issue, as handling different preferences are more expensive, than a homogeneous population is an explanation for original prosperity.

The Role of Religion

Many institutions and norms trace their conception back to religion, and indeed protestant religion have been argued to matter greatly for growth,[26] while the demand for religion also falls with income.[27] Religion also matters for political preferences and long-term stability of institutions some evidence suggest.[28]

[26] J. Bradford De Long, "Productivity Growth, Convergence, and Welfare: Comment", *The American Economic Review*, 78:5 (1988), pp. 1138–1154.

[27] Martin Paldam & Erich Gundlach, "The Religious Transition. A Long-Run Perspective", *Public Choice*, 156:1/2 (2013), pp. 105–123.

[28] Christoph Basten & Frank Betz, "Beyond Work Ethic: Religion, Individual, and Political Preferences", *American Economic Journal: Economic Policy*, 5:3 (2013), pp. 67–91; Robert D. Woodberry, "The Missionary Roots of Liberal Democracy", *American Political Science Review*, 106:2 (2012), pp. 244–274; See Elena Nikolova, & Jakub

	Disposable Income, k		Change in %
	1994	2020	1994-2020
Couples			
Non-manual workers in private sector with 2 children in daycare, rented accommodation	335.900	544.900	62,2
Pensioner couple, each with median private pension, 70 years of age, owner occupied housing	156.300	243.400	55,8
Executive family wih 2 children in daycare, owner occupied housing	500.300	764.600	52,8
Non-manual workers in private sector with 2 children in daycare, owner occupied housing	359.700	531.000	47,6
Pensioner couple with an ATP, no private pension, rented accommodation	131.300	187.800	43
Pensioner couple with an ATP, no private pension, owner occupied housing	150.700	204.700	35,9
LO-couple with 2 children in daycare, rented accommodation	277.200	373.600	34,8
Couple receiving cash benefits with 2 children in daycare, rented accommodation	163.500	209.700	28,3
LO-couple with 2 children in daycare, owner occupied housing	293.600	359.300	22,4
LO-couple, no children, owner occupied housing	303.300	364.200	20,1
Couple receiving integration cash benefits with 2 children in daycare, rented accommodation	163.500	143.000	-12,5
Singles			
Executive, no children, owner occupied housing	316.000	487.300	54,2
Pensioner with median private pension, 70 years of age, rented accommodation	83.700	120.800	44,4
Non-manual worker, no children, owner occupied housing	175.400	250.200	42,6
Pensioner with ATP, no private pension, rented accommodation	83.700	116.900	39,7
Pensioner with ATP, no private pension, owner occupied housing	95.500	125.600	31,5
Person receiving cash benefits, no children, 30+ years old, rented accommodation	55.700	72.000	29,3
LO-employee, no children, rental accommodation	129.600	167.500	29,3
Student not living with parents, rental accommodation, with part-time job	64.000	82.200	28,3
LO-employee, no children, owner occupied housing	136.800	155.400	13,6
Person on unemployment benefits, 25+ years old, no children, rental accommodation	83.800	93.700	11,8
Student not living with parents, rental accommodation, no part-time job	29.000	28.700	-1
Person receiving cash benefits, no children, under 30 years old, rented accommodation	55.700	41.400	-25,6
Person receiving integration cash benefits, no children, 30+ years old, rental accommodation	55.700	32.300	-42,1
Person on unemployment benefits, under 25 years old, no children, rental accommodation	94.600	41.900	-55,7

Fig. 4.8 Development of available spending power after daycare and living expenses for common family types (*Note* Based on the Ministry of Finance Family Type Model. In 1994 immigrants received regular benefits, not the later introduced specific and reduced scheme [integrationsydelse]. The age bracket for under 30 was slightly different in 1994. Students with work has pre-tax wages of 90.000 DKK in the model. *Source* Finansministeriet and CEPOS)

Religion and modern Danish society is a complex issue to disentangle. On the one hand the country was highly religiously uniform under the Lutheran state church in the twentieth century with over 85% of the populace members at the end of the twentieth century—likely above 90%

Polansky. "Conversionary Protestants Do Not Cause Democracy", *British Journal of Political Science*, 51:4 (2021), pp. 1723–1733, for a recent critique of Woodburry's findings.

at the beginning.[29] Also, the role of Christian values is a recurrent theme in public debates, often coupled with a fear of Islam, the religion dominant among non-western immigrants. On the other hand, few Danes are actively religious—only about 10% of the populace reports being in contact with the Church on a weekly basis.

Political theorist Robert H. Nelson has put forward an explanation of the phenomenon and the relation of Lutheranism to the modern Danish economy.[30] His thesis argues that Social democratism has taken over as a form of secularized Lutheranism. It is important to understand that Nelson separates the Calvinist protestant movements that inspired Max Webers famous work on Protestantism[31] and the Lutheran theology largely ignored by Weber.[32] Calvinist ideas were distinctively more pro-market and secularization, where Luther highlighted the obedience to the state authority as essential. Another view is that, the shared Lutheran religion and its close ties with the state authority might be an antecedent of the trust needed to support a welfare state, as argued above. There is clearly indication that can lend merit to the link between a dominant Lutheran heritage and twentieth century economic policy choices, both historically and sociologically.

Historically the welfare state has taken over many services before provided by civil organization, such as religious organizations. Sociologically, the Social Democratic party can be argued to resemble a religion to some extent. It is rife with rituals and symbols, holds the 1st of May as a quasi-religious holiday and to many party-membership is a scared life choice not much affected by whatever the current policy or who the elected officials are. The whole labor market also poses an interest economic conundrum that Lutheranism could help explain; Kleven[33] has

[29] In 2020 the number was just below 75%. See https://www.km.dk/folkekirken/kirkestatistik/folkekirkens-medlemstal, Accessed Jan 25, 2022.

[30] Nelson, *Lutheranism and the Nordic Spirit of Social Democracy: A Different Protestant Ethic.*

[31] Max Weber & Stephen Kalberg, *The Protestant Ethic and the Spirit of Capitalism* (New York: Routledge, 2012).

[32] David Cowan, "Review of 'Lutheranism and the Nordic Spirit of Social Democracy: A Different Protestant Ethic' 'by Robert H. Nelson'", *Journal of Markets & Morality*, 22:2 (2019).

[33] Henrik Jacobsen Kleven, "How can Scandinavians Tax so Much?", *Journal of Economic Perspectives*, 28:4 (2014), pp. 77–98.

shown that in average the net gain for joining the labor force in Scandinavia is around 20% (the US number is 67%), which would make the large labor participation rate irrational for a "homo economicus" worker. However, if work is partly a religious calling to fulfill a purpose this could form part of the explanation.

There is also an interesting aspect of Lutheran heritage in the Danish debate surrounding national sovereignty. As political theories will tell us, modern states are characterized by slicing out sovereignty into various levels such as individual, municipal, federal, and international. This was also to a degree the case in Luther's time and part of his Reformation was a rejection of papal supremacy and also, but less so, the authority of the Holy Roman Emperor. While these institutions had their faults and were largely, particularly the Catholic church, degenerated and corrupt at the time of Luther, both had also in their times served as international bodies of mitigation helping to limit conflict. However, the Danish populace skepticism of divesting sovereignty to international bodies, like the 1992 rejection by referendum of the Maastricht treaty, might also trace back to a fundamentally *national* Lutheranism. Ideas surrounding nationalism, with an emphasis on the common people, and Lutheranism in Denmark has been further investigated by Østergaard.[34]

In Lutheran theology which emphasize salvation by grace as oppose to by work, one of the few requirements of the believers is that they bestow the gift of baptism on their infants. This is in many ways mirrored since 1968 in the Danish State where babies within seconds of birth are given a social security number (a name can wait 6 months). They are admitted into the heaven of welfare on the one hand, but on the other hand the redistributive state would not be able to function nearly to the degree it does without the total dominance of the CPR system. The general unquestioned acceptance of this state baptism might be explained by a Lutheran heritage too.

As a philosopher, Luther also exemplifies Danish society in that he was skeptical of markets and often struggled with the consequences, both

[34] Uffe Østergaard, "Lutheranism, Nationalism and the Universal Welfare State: National Churches and National Identity After the Reformation and the Development of the Welfare State in the Nordic National States", In: Katharina Kunter & Jens Holger Schjørring (ed.), *Europäisches und globales Christentum: Herausforderungen und Transformationen im 20. Jahrhundert* (Göttingen: Vandenhoeck & Ruprecht, 2011), pp. 78–101.

intended and unintended, of his ideas. Luther feared the market, but at the same time had to recognize its potential. In fact, his own stomach was filled largely by his highly entrepreneurial wife Katharina von Bora (1499–1552). The mirror in this of Danish economic policy is uncanny. Danish politicians and the general population are fearful of the market and seek to regulate it, while also understanding that it must be as free as possible to generate enough surplus for redistribution.

Furthermore, it should be mentioned, as Kahl points out; the legacy of Luther was that work itself became a good.[35] This on the one hand propels growth and prosperity, but on the other hand ignores the marginal revolution insight of subjective value and efficient resource distribution generated by the profit motive. This might be at the heel of why many Danish people do not see the relevance of net-tax payer arguments, as recipients of welfare and people employed by the public sector pays taxes on paper (in reality, they cipher some of their cost back into the system). Economist like consequences, politicians talk about intentions, here the Lutheran heritage might play an odd hand in Danish policy perception.

I have attempted to present the Lutheran-heritage explanation as an interesting perspective, however it is at best part of a larger picture and likely not the dominant explanation, as several types of criticism can be raised against it. Firstly, it is hard to pinpoint and indeed match actual historical events to the thesis. Secondly, while Nelson does a fair job of aligning the theology of Luther to the universal welfare state in its Danish guise, it is a stretch. Luther could never have imagined a system like a welfare state, and therefore we cannot answer questions that are core to both his theology and modern economics; particularly relating to motivations, what constitutes truly needy, representative democratic outcomes, etc. Thirdly, as Luther is both a defender of individual consciousness and state authority, he is hard to use for the main questions plaguing a universal welfare state; what should constitute the limits of state expansion into society and the life of individuals? It is also doubtful if Social Democratism has truly taken over from Lutheranism, as so many people still opt to pay church tax—the only truly voluntary tax in Denmark.

[35] Sigrun Kahl, "The Religious Roots of Modern Poverty Policy: Catholic, Lutheran, and Reformed Protestant Traditions Compared", *Archives Européennes de Sociologie/European Journal of Sociology/Europäisches Archiv für Soziologie* (2005), pp. 91–126.

The Romerian Explanation

While 2018 Nobel laureate in economics Paul Romer has not to this authors knowledge ever expressively commented on the antecedent of Danish prosperity, his famous growth theory is a highly relevant explanation for the growth of Danish Prosperity and also aligns well with the concept of innovism. Romer's theory builds on the foundation that economic incentives matter. If people are free to pursue opportunities, they will do so. Particularly he argues that while physical resources, like land, capital, and labor are finite in their use, the ideas that tell us how to utilize these resources are infinite in their use.[36] Hence in a free, meritocratic economy bright minds will seek out and implement ideas and cause innovation. Ideas are unique goods in that they are nonrival, and that they get increasing return to scale, unlike most other economic goods. This means that if an economy, like the Danish, is open, entrepreneurs can seek ideas globally and try them out nationally.

The theory is particularly relevant for the Danish case because, Denmark from 1814 was a resource poor country, but one that was increasingly open to innovations. The diminished military status made the country nonthreatening, while still being considered a robust institutional backdrop likely to last, at least from 1870s. This had several consequences for aspiring Danish business people. They often went abroad to get ideas, like Jacob Christian Jacobsen (1811–1887) the founder of Carlsberg who on travels aboard got inspired by Baverian beer production.[37] Early Danish business people also got invited to spearhead commercial opportunities often as a safe compromise between national interests and lacking national aptitude. A famous example is the C. F. Tietgen run Great Northern Telegraph Company winning bid to lay the trans-Siberian telegraph line.[38]

A key idea of Romer is that good ideas spread. Hence, it is not needed for every businessman to go out of Denmark and pick up the

[36] Paul M. Romer, "Endogenous Technological Change", *Journal of Political Economy*, 98 (1990), pp. 71–102; Charles I. Jones, "Paul Romer: Ideas, Nonrivalry, and Endogenous Growth", *The Scandinavian Journal of Economics*, 121:3 (2019), pp. 859–883.

[37] Fellman et al., *Creating Nordic Capitalism: The Business History of a Competitive Periphery*.

[38] Ole Lange, *Stormogulen: C.F. Tietgen - en finansmand, hans imperium og hans tid 1829–1901* (Copenhagen: Gyldendal, 2006).

idea for new products or processes, rather they can learn from each other. This is very likely what happened and was indeed promoted from mid-nineteenth century to today's government business' schemes emphasis on best practice and educational efforts—both private and public.

The Romer theory is very interesting as it explains the economic miracle of the small resource poor nation very well as an institutional arrangement favorable to endogenous growth. This is not uncontroversial; and the devil is in the detail. If true, the uniquely Danish contribution was the intuitions of free markets put in place long before the welfare state. If this is true, the key to long-term Danish prosperity is to allow and promote entrepreneurs driven by profit to actively search for new ideas—this process is at odds with both detail market regulation and a large public sector economy. In fact, a large public sector might create perverse profit incentives, for instance, for employment, rather than Romerian discovery.

Conclusion

In this chapter, I have collected some, at times competing, at times complementary, explanations for Danish Prosperity. That Danish Capitalism is a result of compromises is a fact. However, the still popular Common People Hypothesis is under severe and deserved attack and likely compromises were not the most optimal path to prosperity that, theoretically, could have been chosen in the twentieth century. Particularly in the later half. Rather new explanations like those advanced by Boje and Romer paints a different narrative that challenges the popular myth of the virtues of a mixed Danish economy, and rather give evidence to the idea of innovism.

CHAPTER 5

The Industrial Denmark in the Twentieth Century

War and Competition—Prelude to the Twentieth Century

Entering the twentieth century, Denmark was predominantly still an agriculturally based nation, with little to no industrial production compared to their European counterparts exemplified in neighboring countries like Germany and Great Britain. While Danish businessmen, factory owners, and industrial innovators weren't late to embrace the ideas of production, coming to the center stage in the Industrial Revolution, the Danish pace were to some extent characterized by a cautious and slow-moving urban and rural development.[1] The real effects and changes in production-thought were first introduced and instigated in Danish rural communities in the 1870–1880s, a full 100 years after its initial inception with the organized machine-based manufacturing industries in Great Britain.[2] This is again testament to the Romerian and innovistic causes of later 20th prosperity as reviewed in Chapter 4.

[1] Thomsen, "Industri, stat og samfund, 1870–1939".

[2] Erik Strange Petersen, "Den økonomiske og sociale udvikling - 1848–1914", In: Steen Busck, Henning Poulsen, & Helge Paludan (eds.), *Danmarks historie - i grundtræk* (Aarhus: Aarhus Universitetsforlag, 2011), pp. 275–279.

© The Author(s), under exclusive license to Springer Nature Switzerland AG 2022

S. K. Sløk-Madsen, *Danish Capitalism in the 20th Century*, Palgrave Studies in Economic History,
https://doi.org/10.1007/978-3-031-04267-6_5

Denmark was lacking access to natural resources, such as the coal mines in Northumberland or the German Ruhr district, which among various things prompted the British and German industrialization in the late-eighteenth and early-nineteenth century, or even the occurrences of natural resources like timber and iron ore as seen in Norway and Sweden, the Danish production and economy were almost entirely based on farming, fishing, and the inland trading of the small scale craftsmanship industries, produced in the privileged market towns (Købstæder).

By the end of the nineteenth century, the European grain-market were overflowed by a steady and ever-growing influx of cheap American grain. The Danish farmers and Western-European farmers alike were easily outcompeted and the Danish agricultural community instead settled on reorganizing its grain production to livestock.[3] The reorganization of grain production to livestock, which required fewer farmhands, combined with emergence of the city-based factories, prompted both the Danish urbanization in the early twentieth century, as well as the reemergence of Danish maritime trade, which had stalled on a mere regional level, since the decline of the Danish colonial empire in the second half of the nineteenth century.[4]

Beside the heavy competition from American grain and the early European manufactories, Denmark was also in some form of an existential crisis after the disastrous Second Schleswig War of 1864 against Prussia and Austria. The peace terms, as cited in the Treaty of Vienna,[5] had reduced Denmark territorially by a one-third and the population with two-fifths to a mere 1.7 million inhabitants. Not only did the forced peace with the Prussians and Austrians dispossess Denmark of a huge chuck of its already sparse population, as well as its arguably most fertile farmlands in the Schleswig–Holstein region of northern Germany, the aftermath of the war had also effectively cut-off the Danish leeway entrance to the Central European markets, leaving Denmark in a economic and political

[3] Carl Erik Andresen & Flemming Agersnap, *Dansk erhvervshistorie 1880 til vore dage* (Copenhagen: Nyt fra Samfundsvidenskaberne, 1989), pp. 9–11.

[4] Lars Jensen, *Danmark – rigsfællesskab,tropekolonier og den postkoloniale arv* (Copenhagen: Hans Reitzels Forlag, 2012), pp. 59–66.

[5] "Frieden-Tractat zwischen Oesterreich, Preußen und Dänemark vom 30. October 1864". Ratified in Vienna November 16, 1864. *Internet Archives*: https://web.archive.org/web/20110719132918/http://www.ambwien.um.dk/NR/rdonlyres/AB922586-4291-44C2-BFFA-0FF1424170A2/0/Fredstraktat1864.pdf, Accessed July 16, 2021.

stalemate compared to its North and Central European counterparts.[6] In fact, commentators at the time should be forgiven for thinking that Denmark was destined for destitution, another of history's victims of poor policy and bad circumstances. It should be noted, that the King Christian IX was likely instrumental in saving Denmark by marrying his offspring into prominent royal houses, earning him the sobriquet father-in-law of Europe.

In addition to the involuntary geopolitical reorientation, Danish entrepreneurs and factory owners were motivated by the nineteenth century Danish liberalization of trade, labor, and civil society, as described in Chapter 2. But regardless of the state's intervention in particular deregulation and liberalization of trade in the 1880s, the business, trade, and commerce of the twentieth century were marked by the turbulence of the last century abroad as well as domestically.

Denmark's decline in terms of foreign affairs, economics, and trade relations in the nineteenth century, initially due to the Napoleonic Wars and later the staggering defeat in 1864, left Denmark in an undesirable status as a small-scale nation, which more or less involuntary contributed to the rearrangement and innovation of the Danish commerce, manufacturers, and merchants in the twentieth century.[7] As we shall see with the birth of the reform agenda in the 1980s onwards, it was also here necessity much more than desire that paved the way for change and market orientation.

For the first time in Danish history, the pursuit and reacquisition of stability, national pride, and prestige weren't left in the hands of the kings and nobles alone, but rather to the manufacturers, merchants, and traders who better than anyone embraced the new national sentiment of idyllic underdogs influenced by the romantic era. Now the people, the folk, and particularly the entrepreneurs had to take action and win an inward struggle to make up for the outward loss of prestige in order to retain national identity, independence, and sovereignty in face of overwhelming

[6] Jens Ole Christensen, "Danske overlevelsesstrategier i skyggen af 1864", In: Inge Adriansen & Steen Bo Frandsen (eds.), *Efter 1864: Krigens følger på kort og langt sigt* (Viborg: Syddansk Universitetsforlag, 2016), pp. 123–124.

[7] Claus Bjørn & Carsten Due-Nielsen,"Fra Helstat til Nationalstat: 1814–1914", In: Carsten Due-Nielsen, Nikolaj Petersen, Ole Feldbæk, Thorsten Borring Olesen, Poul Villaume, Bo Lidegaard, Claus Bjørn et al., *Dansk udenrigspolitiks historie*, Vol. 3 (Copenhagen, Danmarks Nationalleksikon, 2006).

odds—this sentiment still to this day reside as an almost mythological conception of Danish self-awareness in the years after the Second Schleswig War.[8]

States Within the State

A characteristic trait among emerging Danish companies in the early twentieth century—lasting until after the end of the Second World War—was both the idea and practical execution of what can be described as a kind of "patriotic" corporate governance and commerce. I tend to use the term patriotic, with an emphasis on the patriotic perception of nationalism, rather than nationalism in its political and ideological conception as seen in the 1920s and 1930s Spain, Italy, and Germany.[9]

It's patriotic because Danish businesses in the first half of the twentieth century influenced and, to some degree substituted the Danish government on key policy features traditionally regarded matters of the national state in areas like: education, public housing, social welfare, trade policy, and even foreign policy. The "patriotism" manifested itself in the business leaders' efforts for a national recovery after a catastrophic century with the military, political, and economic humiliations from neighboring Sweden[10] and Germany.[11] Put differently, business leaders saw it as their inherent responsibility to resume national business activities, as the state was constantly in turmoil and the callow democratic parliamentarism had acted recklessly and inefficiently since the introduction of democratic reforms in the mid-to-late 1800s.[12]

[8] Nevers, *Det produktive samfund: seks kapitler af industrialiseringens idéhistorie.*

[9] Erik Rasmussen, *Danmarks historie: Velfærdsstaten på vej. 1913–1939.*

[10] Ole Feldbæk, "Tiden 1720–1814", In: Carsten Due-Nielsen, Nikolaj Petersen, Ole Feldbæk, Thorsten Borring Olesen, Poul Villaume, Bo Lidegaard, Claus Bjørn et al., *Dansk udenrigspolitiks historie*, Vol. 2 (Copenhagen, Danmarks Nationalleksikon, 2002).

[11] Carl Grimberg, "Den dansk-tyske Krig 1864", In: Ragner Svanström, Sven Tito Achen, & Kai Petersen (ed.), *Grimbergs Verdenshistorie – Bismarcks Epoke*, Vol. 15 (Copenhagen: Politikens Forlag, 1968), pp. 45–50.

[12] Mørch, *25 statsministre: 25 fortællinger om magten i Danmark i det tyvende århundrede*, pp. 17–22.

On the one hand, they wanted to re-establish the traditional Danish trade both locally in the Oresund region,[13] as well as the long trade connections to East Asia and America. In the local sphere, Danish merchants had a monopolistic advantage in the Oresund trade, due to the strict Danish mercantilism personified in the despised Oresund's customs (Øresundstolden), for which maritime trade between the North Sea and the rich market towns of Prussia, Poland, Sweden, and Russia had filled the coffins of the Danish state with foreign currency from the late-Middle Ages until its abolition in 1857.[14]

In terms of global trade, the Danish merchants had for generations held a foothold in both transatlantic trade and the East Asian trade networks, due to Danish colonization in the seventeenth century.[15] By the year 1900, Danish control of the maritime enclaves in India and the African Gold Coast had ceased, while Danes retained control of its West Indian possessions at Saint Croix, Saint John, and Saint Thomas until 1917, when the islands were sold to the United States for 25 million dollars and later renamed the US Virgin Islands.[16] The companies' starting point for a relaunch of Danish trade and commerce could thus be based on both a local and a global network, with long traditions of Danish trade presence among the Western-European players.

Danish industry and companies have commonly been based on three different origins, (1) craftsman from the Jutlandic heath like LEGO, founded in Billund in 1932,[17] (2) privileged market towns like such as Svendborg where Maersk were founded in 1904,[18] or (3) the Copenhagen-based establishment of financiers with close ties to the

[13] Also commonly known as The Sound, Oresund is one of the four waterways linking the Baltic Sea with the North Sea. Beside the waterway in Oresund, the danes also held control of the straits; Great and the Little Belt, dominating the seagoing trade until the Kiel Canal in Schleswig–Holstein was completed in 1895.

[14] Kalevi Ahonen: "Den dansk-amerikanske strid om Øresundstolden", In: Ole Degn (ed.), *Tolden i Sundet: toldopkrævning, politik og skibsfart i Øresund 1429–1857* (Copenhagen: Told- og Skattehistorisk Selskab, 2010).

[15] Gerda Bonderup, "Reformer: Enevælden i praksis", In: Steen Busck, Henning Poulsen, & Helge Paludan (eds.), *Danmarks historie - i grundtræk* (Aarhus: Aarhus Universitetsforlag, 2011), p. 210.

[16] Ove Hornby, *Kolonierne i Vestindien* (Copenhagen: Politiken, 1980).

[17] Niels Lunde, *Miraklet i LEGO* (Copenhagen: Gyldendal, 2013), p. 264.

[18] Bo Lidegaard, *En fortælling om Danmark i det 20. århundrede* (Copenhagen: Gyldendal, 2011), p. 36.

Fig. 5.1 Meeting among Financiers. Original title: "Et møde blandt finansmænd". 1904. August Jerndorff (1846–1906). Pictured is the board of ØK in a meeting with CEO of Landmandsbanken Isak Glückstadt (1839–1910) far left, then H. N. Andersen (1852–1937), admiral du Plessis de Richelieu (1852–1932), CEO of Privatbanken Axel Heide (1861–1915), and in a very comfortable laid-back position the law, the capital, academia and the policy personified in professor and council president (Prime Minister) Johan Henrik Deuntzer (1845–1918)

governmental institution and the Danish royal family, as exemplified with the East Asiatic Company (Danish: Det Østasiatiske Kompagni or simply *ØK*), founded in 1897[19] (Fig. 5.1).

[19] Martin Iversen, *Udsyn – ØK, Danmark og verden* (Copenhagen: Lindhardt og Ringhof, 2016), pp. 68–69.

It is especially the Copenhagen-based companies, closely linked to the both the parliamentary and the aristocratic establishment like the East Asiatic Company (EAC), who were the first to embrace the tenets of patriotic corporate governance and commerce. The EAC was a founded as a trading company, originally focused on the lucrative trade of transporting teak from Southeast Asia, but later branched out its activities to include trade and maritime transportation on a global scale.

The company's backers were a section of the very elite of Danish society among other; J.H. Deuntzer (1845–1918), a prominent law professor who later became Prime Minster,[20] Andreas du Plessis de Richelieu (1852–1932), a Danish admiral employed in the Siamese fleet, the bank managers of Denmark's two largest banks *Landmandsbanken* and *Privatbanken*, represented, respectively, by Isak Glückstadt (1839–1919) and Axel Heide (1861–1915) and last but not least, the primary founder and CEO of the EAC H.N. Andersen (1852–1937), who himself were closely connected to the royal houses of Denmark, Russia, and the United Kingdom.[21] Andersen's close ties with the Danish and both European aristocratic power elite, proved not surprisingly to have significant advantages in the operations in the early years of the EAC, but also in the influence of the policies pursued by the Danish government.

An early but decisive example of Andersen's and EAC's influence on the Danish state can be found in the board's active involvement, and even in some cases, directly dictating the Danish foreign policy during the First World War.[22] At the outbreak of war in 1914, Denmark was a neutral state, or rather, a semi-neutral state. While Denmark was not directly involved in the acts of war between the Entente Powers[23] or the Central Powers,[24] Denmark's straits and waterway's strategic location between the Baltic Sea and the North Sea was a recurring diplomatic battle for the

[20] Søren Mørch, *25 statsministre: 25 fortællinger om magten i Danmark i det tyvende århundrede*, pp. 31–34.

[21] Flemming Højbo, *Det sidste Kompagni: ØKs storhed og fald* (Albertslund: J.H. Schultz, 1993), pp. 22–24.

[22] Bent Blüdnikow, "Denmark during the First World War", *Journal of Contemporary History*, 24:4 (1989), pp. 683–703.

[23] United Kingdom, France, Serbia, the Russian Empire, Italy, Japan, and the United States.

[24] Germany, Austria-Hungary, Bulgaria, and the Ottoman Empire.

Admiralties in Berlin and London—in 1916 in fact the largest naval battle of the war was waged of the Danish coast of Jutland.

For Denmark itself, the war was a fine balance between being able to profit from the war, as well as avoid provoking the warring great powers. The Danish business owners and farmers in particular favored neutrality as Germany and Great Britain waged a war of starvation against each other, and thus the Danish merchant ships could profit on an almost exclusive right to trade in the submarine-infested waters.[25] In Berlin, the German diplomats put pressure on and succeeded in persuading the Danish government to mine the Danish sound and belts, while the British First Lord of the Admiralty, Winston Churchill (1874–1965), made great efforts to persuade the War Cabinet in London to justify a preventive invasion of Denmark to secure the food supply chain, as well as avoiding the continued dominance of the Central Powers in Oresund and the Baltic Sea.[26] Denmark, meanwhile, avoided an invasion by both the Entente Powers and the Central Powers, and maintained their neutrality throughout the war.[27]

The fact that Denmark maintained its neutrality can be attributed, among other things, to the active involvement and influence of major business owners in the Danish government. Here again, I would like to highlight H.N. Andersen's role as a shadow politician as an example of the archetype of contemporary society's mix of businessmen and self-employed civil servants. Andersen had, like most Danes at the outbreak of the war, an Anglophile sentiment. The war in 1864 still hung heavily in the air, and the anti-German convictions were evident in all sections of the population, but the war also meant that companies like the EAC potentially could lose all of its export business, effectively their entire market. Danish neutrality was therefore crucial for Danish companies if they were

[25] Bo Lidegaard, "Overleveren: 1914–1945", In: Carsten Due-Nielsen, Nikolaj Petersen, Ole Feldbæk, Thorsten Borring Olesen, Poul Villaume, Bo Lidegaard, Claus Bjørn et al., *Dansk udenrigspolitiks historie*, Vol. 4 (Copenhagen, Danmarks Nationalleksikon, 2006).

[26] Jørgen Sevaldsen, *Churchill – Statsmand og myte* (Copenhagen: Lindhardt og Ringhof, 2012), pp. 83–88.

[27] Nils Arne Sørensen, *Den store krig: Europæernes første verdenskrig* (Copenhagen: Gad, 2019).

to survive to the end of the war without significant sacrifices, and therefore the Danish business community itself had to ensure that the right foreign and trade policy was implemented.

The Danish Foreign Affairs Minister Erik Scavenius (1877–1962)[28] himself showed up at EAC's headquarters a few weeks after the outbreak of the war and urged Andersen to use his high-ranking contacts in the Russian, British and German royal houses to preserve peace—an offer that Andersen could not refuse.[29] A senior official of King George V's court, sir Arthur Davidson (1856–1922), gave during the war, a characteristic of H.N. Andersen in a letter, to the British envoy in Saint Petersburg: "*He has an exceptional knowledge of the general internal politics of England, Russia and Germany and of the forces influencing it. He is probably the only living person who has spoken openly to the German Emperor since the war broke out. He knows the Tsar who - I think - trusts him and believes in his honesty as much as the kings of England and Denmark.*"[30] Of course, having Andersen's connections was extraordinary for his time as well as it would be today, but the fact that leading Danish financiers and in the first half of the twentieth century actively influenced and supported government roles was not unusual.

Andersen would make use of his contacts in Berlin, informing the Germans that the Danish waters would be mined, as requested by the German high command at the outbreak of war. At the same time, he would inform his contacts in London without the Germans knowing, that the Danish mines were not armed, thus setting the stage for the delicate and risky play of Danish neutrality during the First World War, instrumented by self-employed civil servants like Andersen.[31]

In addition to the involvement of trade and foreign policy as seen in the example of the First World War, which also can be argued to be solely in the EAC's self-interest, one should also point out the culture and

[28] Minister of Foreign Affairs 1909–1910, 1913–1920, 1940–1943 and Prime Minister from 1942 to 1945. On this see Viggo Sjøqvist, *Erik Scavenius: Danmarks udenrigsminister under to verdenskrige: statsminister 1942–1945* (Copenhagen: Gyldendal, 1973).

[29] Iversen, *Udsyn – ØK, Danmark og verden*, p. 218.

[30] Højbo, *Det sidste Kompagni: ØKs storhed og fald*, p. 30.

[31] Knud J.V. Jespersen, *Rytterkongen: et portræt af Christian 10* (Copenhagen: Gyldendal, 2009), pp. 210–215.

interest of companies in supporting and taking measures in social policies, which today is considered matters and responsibilities of the state.[32] It is especially with the companies' active interest and contribution to the Danish education sector, that we find numerous examples of the patriotic corporate governance and commerce.

In Denmark, compulsory education was introduced in 1814, based on the Enlightenment ideals and thus all children aged 7–14 should undergo a basic education in reading, spelling, mathematics, and the teaching of Christ.[33] After finishing school, the 13–14-year olds were in many ways on their own, and in most cases the children were expected to work at their family's craft, which often had been the case for generations. Further education after the age of 14 was only in the form of apprenticeship and had traditionally belonged to the trades of agriculture, carpentry, masonry, blacksmiths, and smaller manufacturing trades such as tailors or cabinetmakers. But in the mid-nineteenth century, corporations and business prompted by the industrialization took over large parts of laborers from the crafts and agricultural class, due to the lack of competent, and above all skilled and loyal employees, of the new urban industrial society.[34]

Companies such as Maersk, Carlsberg, the EAC and later Novo Nordisk, Bang and Olufsen (B&O), and LEGO were all founders of an educational trend[35] in which children and young adults, who after completing their basic education, took on the responsibility and the financing of further education for thousands of Danes, who later became lifelong employees.[36] The motivation of the business community was twofold, on the one hand they wanted the qualified labor for themselves,

[32] Michael Kuur Sørensen, "Alle elsker velfærdsstaten?", In: Sissel Bjerrum Fossat, Rasmus Glenthøj, & Lone Kølle Martinsen (eds.), *Konfliktzonen Danmark: Stridende fortællinger om dansk historie* (Copenhagen: Gads Forlag, 2018).

[33] "Kong Frederik den Siettes allernaadigste Forordninger og aabne Breve for Aar 1814". Dated July 27, 1814. *Danmarkshistorien.dk*: https://danmarkshistorien.dk/fileadmin/filer/Billeder/Scanninger_af_kilder/Forordning_om_Skolerne_paa_Landet_i_Danmark__23._januar_1739/Forordning_om_Skolerne_paa_Landet_i_Danmark__23._januar_1739..compressed.pdf, pp. 237–264, Accessed Aug 9, 2021.

[34] Carl Erik Andresen & Flemming Agersnap, *Dansk erhvervshistorie 1880 til vore dage* (Copenhagen: Nyt fra Samfundsvidenskaberne, 1989), pp. 31–38.

[35] Erik Strange Petersen, *Det unge demokrati – 1841–1901* (Aarhus: Institut for Kultur og Samfund, 2014), p. 43.

[36] Højbo, *Det sidste Kompagni: ØKs storhed og fald*, p. 17.

and on the other hand it was obvious to them that the early modern state wasn't able to provide a satisfactory extension of the basic compulsory education. It is a matter for future debate if indeed they even favored a state role in this.

Throughout the nineteenth century, companies and wealthy individuals had also made up a considerable part of the financing of other welfare areas, such as poverty relief and contributions to public health care. The adoption of the constitution in 1849 was the starting point for what was to become a Danish welfare state with some universal benefits, e.g., the provisions of the constitution ensure that poverty relief, to the worthy needy, was secured as a fundamental right.[37] The challenge, however, was that the state did not have the means to support the welfare policy from the beginning, which is why companies and individuals acted as philanthropic benefactors, who at the same time dictated the provisions for whom and on what conditions the poverty benefits could be provided.[38]

The companies from the Copenhagen-based establishment, such as the EAC, were particularly dominant in the first part of the twentieth century, up until the Second World War. This is mainly due to their close ties and hence the influence on both the old aristocracy and the early democratic institutions. But what made these "elite" companies rich and powerful in Denmark and abroad before World War II can be argued to be what also caused their decline after World War II.

Domestically, the German occupation of Denmark (April 9, 1940–May 5, 1945) meant the companies' close ties with both the aristocratic and democratic power elite effectively got cut off with the dissolution of the Danish parliament in 1943 Since it has not played the same role in the direct influence of the policy pursued, which is characteristic of the patriotic corporate governance and commerce of the late 1800s to mid-1900s.[39] The post-war period also slowly dissolved the remnants of the past imperialist world hegemony and gave rise to independence of the former European colonies around the globe in the 1940s, 1950s, and 1960s which meant that companies like the EAC had to reform their

[37] Den grundlovgivende rigsforsamling, "Danmarks Riges Grundlov, 5. juni 1849".

[38] Ida-Elisabeth Andersen & Dorrit Pedersen, *Gamlesagen: Mellem filantropi og velfærdsstat – Ensomme gamles værn 1910–2020* (Copenhagen: Fonden Ensommes Gamles Værn, 2020).

[39] Claus Bundgård Christensen, *Danmark besat: krig og hverdag 1940–45* (Copenhagen: Gyldendals Bogklubber, 2009).

raison d'être and approach to trading if they were to succeed in entering a global world increasingly based on free trade capitalism—they were to reform or to decline.

The Allied liberation of Denmark in May 1945, the late-1940s reconstruction of the democratic institutions and the European Recovery Programs (ERP) introduction of general American-style capitalism marked the end of the patriotic corporate governance and commerce and instead installed a new era of business mentally in Denmark which where to continue throughout the twentieth century and until today. It wasn't an insignificant proportion of Danish companies from this particular era, who stated as acting as these plutocratic "states" within the Danish state, who freely and willingly functioned as autonomous state-agents and eventually capitalized on this ideological patriotic foundation. Several Danish companies managed to reform in the new style of global capitalism and went on to become business-empires in their own right through the twentieth century. Nevertheless the tendency of patriotic corporate governance and commerce which can be spotted among numerous companies founded in the early-to-mid twentieth century, can be described as being the very bedrock of Danish enterprise.[40]

Innovation and the New Schools of Thought

The Danish post-war experience is in most aspects different than their European counterparts in Germany, Poland, Great Britain, and France. In terms of economics, the Nazi-occupation had taken its toll on Danish enterprise, but not even in the slightest degree similar to what went on in the Netherlands, Belgium, or even neighboring Norway, countries that were also subjugated by the Nazi-occupation. The Danes had, to put it mildly, a comparably soft occupation with little significant or lasting damages to housing or infrastructure.[41]

During the war the Danish government had practiced the now infamous *appeasement* or *cooperation policy* (samarbejdspolitik), which essentially can be described as the state's acceptance of a peaceful Nazi-German

[40] Bertel Bernhard, *Sådan skabtes Danmarks store virksomheder* (Aarhus: Erhvervs-Bladets Forlag, 1988).

[41] Vilhelm La Cour, *Danmark under Besættelsen*, Vols. 1–3 (Copenhagen, Westermann, 1947); Hansen," Økonomisk vækst i Danmark: 1720–1914".

occupation, in return for keeping certain liberties.[42] The Danish cooperation policy has widely been criticized after the war, both abroad as well as domestically, accusing the Danish wartime government of encouraging further collaboration with Nazi Germany and for keeping the Nazi warmachine well feed and well supplied throughout the war.[43] The practical outcome of the cooperation policy did however result in not having to deal with a major internal refugee crises and resurrection of both housing and critical infrastructure.[44]

The Nazi-occupation of Denmark was not without its hardships: exploitations, censorship, and fatal mock-trails as seen in other Nazi-occupied territories of Europe. But relatively, compared to the rest of the occupied countries of Europe, the Nazi-occupation of Denmark was characterized by general relative undisturbed peacefulness (particularly early on), and Danish society could in most cases resume its activities in the days after the liberation on May 5, 1945.

Immediately after the Second World War, Denmark sought to stay out of the beginning bloc division of the world, spearheaded by the United States in the West and the USSR in the East. After a failed attempt to create a defense alliance with Norway and Sweden in 1948,[45] the same year, the Danish Parliament gave way that Denmark would accept the

[42] Henning Poulsen, *Besættelsesårene 1940–1945* (Aarhus: Aarhus Universitetsforlag, 2002).

[43] Hans Kirchhoff, *Samarbejde og modstand under besættelsen: en politisk historie*, 2nd ed. (Odense: Syddansk Universitetsforlag, 2004).

[44] The social foundation of the antecedents to the modern Danish welfare state, instituted in 1933, had been ongoing throughout the war and cannot be pointed out to be disturbed by the war, in any major degree either. Thus, people were still receiving benefits, the children were still learning read and write in the schools, and the doctors and nurses were still tending to the sick and vulnerable. The unions and labor-movements were also still active during the war as a part of the compromise of the cooperation policy, as was political parties still legally operation, with the exception of the Danish Communist Party. That said, Venstre did pursue illiberal policies of a light reintroduction of Stavnsbåndet for unwed farmhands under 30, a potential work conscription and even loss of voting rights for welfare recipients in 1941. The actual effect of these policies is not clear. They were pursued, as Venstre at the time was worried about the effect of social benefits on work ethics and the worry that people abused the benefits.

[45] Henrik S. Nissen, *Nordens historie: 1397–1997: 10 essays* (Oslo: Norsk rikskringkasting, 1997); Bengt Sundelius & Claes Wiklund, *Norden i sicksack: tre spårbyten inom nordiskt samarbete* (Stockholm: Santérus, 2000).

offer to receive American support through George C. Marshall's brainchild, the ERP. A year later, in 1949, Denmark would join NATO as one of its founding members, solidifying the Danish position well within the Western bloc.[46]

While many companies had survived the war, Danish companies were largely characterized by a stubbornly stagnant business life and primitive production methods in second half of the 1940s, a tendency not only seen in Denmark, but on most of the European continent.[47] Europe's great distress in addition to the damage of the war was the lack of innovation and capital, which otherwise had been flowing since the beginning decades of the nineteenth century.[48] Particularly Germany had in the interwar years been a pioneer of innovation, now that motor was torn asunder.[49] Denmark and Danish production and industry thus lacked both in the form of economic resources, but also a renewed willingness to innovate in both products and conducts of commerce.[50] Despite the general hardships of the war, the Danish production apparatus was intact, and the massive destruction across the European continent constitutes a massive demand, also for Danish labor and production. But the Danish production apparatus was also relatively obsolete. During the late 1940s, the surrounding countries rebuilt large parts of their industry, while Denmark's production did not experience the same development, and with the devaluation of the pound in 1949, the Danish industry was pressured even further. For Danish manufacturers and commerce, the governments' active involvement in the ERP was of monumental importance.

Out of the total 13 billion that made up the ERP, Denmark and Danish companies received $ 305 million (Equivalent to $ 3.4 billion in 2021 exchange rates), of which $ 33 million was in the form of

[46] Robert Watt Boolsen, *Danmark og NATO gennem 40 år: Atlantsammenslutningen 4. april 1989* (Copenhagen: Atlantsammenslutningen, 1989).

[47] Peter Termin, "The Golden Age of European Growth Reconsidered", *European Review of Economic History*, 6:1 (2002), pp. 3–22.

[48] Tamás Vonyó, "Reconstruction After Two World Wars: Why a Difference", *Journal of European Economic History*, 30 (2001), pp. 429–458.

[49] Peter Hayes, *Industry and Ideology: IG Farben in the Nazi Era* (Cambridge: Cambridge University Press, 1987).

[50] Jeppe Nevers, "Capitalism in Times of Crisis: Danish Industrialists and the State, c. 1910–1940", *Scandinavian Journal of History*, 44:5 (2019), pp. 552–571.

loans.[51] The US dollar subsidy provided a much-needed helping hand to the crisis-stricken Danish economy, which lacked foreign currency to initiate imports. In addition to increasing imports of American raw materials, metals, and technology in particular, the funds were also intended to strengthen Danish companies' technology and product innovation and the Danish government was strongly encouraged by the United States to let the state coordinate and plan investments to promote the country's industrialization.[52]

I would argue that the recovery of the European economy after the Second World War is one of the greatest achievements of the twentieth century, which was largely due to the efforts of the United States in the years after the war. From a Danish perspective, it first and foremost dismantled the pseudo-plutocracy of the past, known from companies such as the EAC, and converted the Danish business management from the previously described patriotic corporate commerce to a regular modern market economy following an American model. The 1950s Danish development in living standards for private individuals and the economic growth for companies is a good example of ERP's long-term positive effects in a microcosm. All this appears as somewhat of an ideological conflict for classical liberalism. However, since wars are caused by states, one can forgive classical liberals for demanding that states also rebuild after were as compensation. This is still a far cry from believing states as required for markets, which is the common argument on the left.

The American subsidies from ERP were not only redistributed to the existing large companies. It also took place in local innovation such as in the form of new tools and implements for farmers. In 1950s, Denmark was still dependent on dozens of day-laborers to help with the annual harvest, the ERP effectively replaced the scythe and day-laborers with American tractors, which meant that there was a need for fewer workers in agriculture, who now instead could venture to the factories of the growing cities.

The ERP also helped elevate the innovation of the smaller craftsman and market towns-companies, who during the 1950s was some of the

[51] Thorsten Borring Olesen & Poul Villaume, "I blokopdelingens tegn 1945–1972", In: Carsten Due-Nielsen, Nikolaj Petersen, Ole Feldbæk, Thorsten Borring Olesen, Poul Villaume, Bo Lidegaard, Claus Bjørn et al., *Dansk udenrigspolitiks historie*, Vol. 5 (Copenhagen, Danmarks Nationalleksikon, 2006).

[52] Ibid.

most visible standard bearers for Danish growth and development. The renewed access to foreign markets provided inspiration and the essential capital for companies such as LEGO, which now chose to abandon its production of wooden toys in favor of investing in the now well-known plastic building blocks, an idea that the business leaders from LEGO adopted after an inspiration trip in England.[53] Another example of Danish innovation can be found at B&O, which after the war had had its factories, in Struer in Central Jutland, laid in ruins as part of German retaliatory operations. At B&O, they chose to be inspired by the development of American radio and television, but instead of making the product available to the general public, they chose to focus on design and quality,[54] which raises the product's price, but at the same time made it more sought after at the wealthy end of the growing foreign market.[55]

This leads to what I would call the general shift between Danish companies' focus to innovation and product development. From 1950 and onwards, we can sketch a business trend which arguably still is ongoing, originating especially with those companies who were favored by economic development programs like ERP. The companies which have thrived both in Denmark and abroad with the stamp "Made in Denmark", their development has either been due to; (1) Danish entrepreneurs' insistence on raising the quality of existing products, i.e., with toys and music, television, and radio systems in the cases of, respectively, LEGO and B&O, or (2) with the practical support of the ordinary workers lifestyle and well-being. Danish business history is rich in examples of distinction between these two "schools of thought" but let us dwell in an example of the latter.[56]

In 1951, civil engineer Aage Louis-Hansen and Johanne Louis-Hansen, a former nurse turned housewife, founded *Dansk Plastic Emballage*, a business focusing manufacturing plastic. While the company's initial purpose was to produce plastic packaging for the growing Danish food industry, their original business-setup was to change in 1954, when

[53] Bernhard, *Sådan skabtes Danmarks store virksomheder.*

[54] Innovation was an integral part of the design process at B&O. For instance, they invented and marketed the wheel changer later used in the Apple's blockbuster Ipod. Unfortunately they rarely—just like in this case—patented they innovation as standalone features, focusing more on the total design and product.

[55] Bernhard, *Sådan skabtes Danmarks store virksomheder.*

[56] i.e. Rockwool, Grundfoss, Danfoss, ISS.

Elise Sørensen, a home nurse, contacted the Louis-Hansen family with both a cry for help and what later would become a revolutionary idea. Sørensen's sister have had an ostomy operation and were afraid to go out in public, fearing that her stoma might leak. Johanne Louis-Hansen knew this weren't a singular case, and as a former nurse she knew of the worries of odor nuisance and stoma leak often experienced by ostomy patients, so when Sørensen requested the company to develop an ostomy-bag for her sister, they recognized the need in the market for disposable ostomy-bags, affordable to the ordinary working-class citizen turned patient.[57]

It was not long before Sørensen's idea was transformed into reality at the plastic manufactory and thus the product development of an ostomy-bag both leak-proof and free of the ordinary nuisances for the patients began. After several years of developing a safe and reliable product, the Louis-Hansen's factory finally succeeded with completing the development of the ostomy-bag *COLOPLAST* in 1957. The demand for the newly developed product was high, not only in the Danish domestic market, already in the early 1960s more than 80% of the company's production was sold to the European market.[58] During the 1970s, the number of ostomy patients in the Western world was estimated at around one million patients, today it's estimated that approximately 1 in 500 Americans live with an ostomy. By the mid-1970s, a vast majority of Western countries had recognized the need to cover the costs in whole or in partly through either private or public health insurance for patients relying on ostomy aids.[59]

Coloplast, as the company had changed its name to in 1957, continued their development of new products for the markets and products considered taboo or marked by social stigma. Based on the knowledge and experience that Coloplast had gained with the product market, for the more or less taboo diseases, as the case with ostomy patients, the company began to expand their production to similar areas. In the 1980s, product development began on aids for urinary incontinence, i.e., persons who have no control over their urination. And in the 1990s, they repeated the

[57] Gry Jexen, *Kvinde kend din historie: spejl dig i fortiden* (Copenhagen: Gyldendal, 2021).

[58] Bernhard, *Sådan skabtes Danmarks store virksomheder*.

[59] Hans-Otto Loldrup. *Dansk medicin: historien om de danske medicinfabrikker* (Copenhagen: Loldrup, 2014).

same formula, this time focusing on aids for people suffering from wound diseases and skin diseases.[60]

By highlighting Coloplast as an example of a Danish company that provides the practical support of an ordinary workers lifestyle and well-being, one should not be blind to the mere fact that Coloplast and companies like it is not only established to do good and supporting distressed patients all over the world out of a kind heart. It is, of course, the benefit of the hard work, the yield of their labors itself that makes enterprising business owners, such as Louis-Hansen, wanting to make an effort. It is an overall commercial thinking and the profit-motive so well-known, and summed up by the iconic quote from Adams Smith's Wealth of Nation: "*It is not from the benevolence of the butcher, the brewer, or the baker that we expect our dinner, but from their regard to their own self-interest*".[61] With many Danish companies so adapt at solving so many different issues, it is odd that the Danish state does not contain more private production of welfare (which can still be funded by redistribution if politically decided).

While the essence of the Smith quote is true and is an unmistakable reality for almost all traders and people striving in commerce, in societies who have embraced the capitalist doctrines of free-market trade, it is at the same time a fact that Danish companies have yielded great prosperity on the basis of the companies' schools of thought and business structures. This is not a distinctive Danish phenomenon, but instead I would argue that it is a phenomenon with a certain Danish over-representation.

The New Origins and Conclusion

From a business historical perspective, Denmark in the twentieth century is a success story. The country went from a country with very little production, to being able to stand the test of international competition, to be the home of competitive export-driven global private sector.[62] The

[60] Bernhard, *Sådan skabtes Danmarks store virksomheder.*

[61] Adam Smith, *An Inquiry into the Nature and Causes of the Wealth of Nations*, R.H. Campbell, A.S. Skinner, W.B. Todd (eds.), Vol. 1 (Indianapolis: Oxford University Press, 1981), pp. 26–27.

[62] Asmussen, "Danmark i kapitalismens guldalder: forholdet mellem den økonomiske politik og den samfundsøkonomiske udvikling i Danmark i 1950'erne".

country thus follows the same development trend as seen in the neighboring Western countries. In this way, the superficial narrative about the development of the Danish business community is not directly distinctive, as previously described. But when you study Denmark's business history more closely, you will still be able to identify special Danish conditions that strengthened the Danish development of companies in the twentieth century. As described in this chapter, Denmark was more or less a pseudo-plutocracy at the turn of the year 1900 and until the end of the Second World War, with wealthy companies both directly and indirectly influencing the governance of the country. After the Second World War, much of the power of these wealthy corporations, whose fortunes and connections were closely linked to colonial and aristocratic connections, was dissolved, and the institutions which made them prosperous did not survive the post-war world of free-market capitalism. The post-war period was marked by growth and prosperity in Denmark, but also in most parts of the Western world. While Denmark also had a share of state-run companies—de facto protected bureaucracies—various Danish governments have been more focused on limiting governments' ownership in companies than in other Western states, which has been good for consumer welfare and competition. Danish people pay some of the relative lowest phone fares, for instance, and the sale of stocks in Dong Energy (now Ørsted) to Goldman Sachs has proven a great deal for the Danish state. As did the bank relief doing the 2008 financial crisis where all loans to the banks was paid back with dividend to the state. How the state-run companies saw the development is another matter—the Danish rail service company DSB has gone from top European fame to the periphery of attention and service.

The small and medium-sized Danish companies, which were originally made up of artisans and craftsmen from the Jutlandic heath or merchants from the privileged market towns, broke the old plutocratic monopoly, a breach I will unequivocally attribute to the emergence of real free competition and free trade. It was this breach of age-old business conducts that in the twentieth century made Denmark prosperous—a process long in the making, but easily jeopardized by later welfare policy.

With the development and prosperity came the specialization of companies. In this chapter, I have chosen to make a cursory division of what I describe as the "two schools of thought", knowing that there are Danish companies that do not uniquely fit into either one of the two framework-descriptions for schools of thought. I am aware that numerous

Danish companies, small and large, will find themselves in the somewhat a gap between these two schools. That being said, it is an attempt to distinguish both the depiction and the development in the post-war period.

Today, there is only one major Danish company left that can be argued to act in the likes of the EAC in modern day Denmark, namely the *A.P. Moller-Maersk Group*, which very similar to EAC has large parts of its operations associated with shipping on the world's oceans. But even Maersk can be pointed out to be quality developers of their core product, as Maersk was the innovator of first purpose-built container vessel in the world, which began operating in 1951.[63]

By the 1990s the old three-way scheme of business origins; the craftsmen from the heath, the privileged market towns, and Copenhagen-based establishment had all faded away. With the rise of globalization, the 1900s artificial business-borders were still harder to find. Denmark is a small country comprised by some few hundred islands extending a mere 16,577 sq. miles (not including Greenland and the Faroese Islands), approximately about half the size of South Carolina. With Denmark's geographical limitations, the traditional business structures eroded and was instead replaced by modern business clusters.[64] These business clusters are groups of corporations who have located themselves in the same economic region because it offers some competitive advantages. It can be related companies that are in the same industry and compete in the same market, which is why they draw on the same regional resources and infrastructure.[65] Denmark being a small country these business clusters often include companies who already rival or collaborate—in both instances

[63] Anders Ravn Sørensen, *Danmark som søfartsnation: fortællinger, interesser og identitet gennem 250 år* (Copenhagen: Gad, 2020).

[64] Niels Boje Groth & Søren Smidt-Jensen, *Erhvervsklynger i den fysiske planlægning: tre eksempelstudier Randers - Herning – Nakskov* (Hørsholm: Skov & Landskab, 2005); Marie Skjold Jørgensen, Louise Marianne Lempel, & Jørgen Rosted, *Danske Erhvervsklynger* (Copenhagen: FORA, 2010).

[65] Some business clusters are more integrated than others. For example, a large representation is seen of the food industry's headquarters in East Jutland and the Pharma industry is mainly located in North Zealand.

furthering their venture, contributing to making them more competitive. Clusters have also changed nature in the twentieth century. The case of Danish fashion comes to mind, from a low cost local production to outsourced global powerhouses like Bestseller and Ecco, the concept of Danish clusters change, as global market change; Denmark is a small nation in a very big world.[66]

[66] Fellman et al., *Creating Nordic Capitalism: The Business History of a Competitive Periphery.*

CHAPTER 6

The Methods and Institutions of Twentieth Century Danish Capitalism

A sometimes-raised critique of institutional economics is the fluffy nature of the terms used. Authors are at risk of painting with a too broad brush as to not convey any meaningful understanding. While detailed study of specific institutions sometimes become closer to law reviews and sever the connection to the overall narrative. Yet most will agree that institutional context and even path dependency of choice set related to institutions and their design matter deeply for both historical and economic outcomes.

While most of this book is dedicated to a broad historical narrative of Danish firm-based capitalism in the twentieth century, it would not be complete without dealing in some detail with some more unique institutions and norms prevalent in Denmark in the twentieth century. For the six chosen, of which three are institutional arrangements; the model of the labor market, and two prevalent ownership-types forms for firms. Two are in the interstice of institution and policy; daycare and the public pension scheme, while the last one is clearly more toward a norm or tradition, Købmandskab—a potential Danish sales approach.

I have attempted to present the selected six phenomenon as descriptively and historically as possible, while also highlighting challenges and potential changes to make the knowledge relevant for a broader audience.

© The Author(s), under exclusive license to Springer Nature Switzerland AG 2022

S. K. Sløk-Madsen, *Danish Capitalism in the 20th Century*, Palgrave Studies in Economic History,
https://doi.org/10.1007/978-3-031-04267-6_6

The Danish Model and Flexicurity

When a student takes an introductory economic class, they will likely walk away with an understanding that output depends largely on the input of labor and capital. While there is more to it (such as technology), there is no denying that labor matter, and flexibility of labor matters greatly. This is particularly true of Denmark with its poor level of natural resources. It is therefore paramount to understand the unique institutional arrangements of the Danish labor market, dubbed Flexicurity by the last Prime Minister of the twentieth century Poul Nyrup Rasmussen. The term highlighting the outcome of a flexible, what economist might call variable or dynamic, workforce, and protection against unemployment. However, the system is often misunderstood internationally.

While the government plays a role[1]—particular in services related to unemployment, the system is at heart a market-based approach to labor relations. It is a voluntary setup between the representative of the employer and employee side. The employers side recognize the workers' rights to organize and seek collective bargaining gains, while the employees side recognize that management has the right to hire, fire and organize the production. Historically the trade unions were tied to the Social Democratic party and they performed an a highly important service in keeping communists and other radicalized workers didn't gain positions of importance and power, which ensured a somewhat friendly negotiation environment.

Furthermore, there is no state-set minimum wage. While there are plenty of regulations that influence daily labor, the area of agreement of terms between employees and employers is largely self-regulated via the Agreement on the Labor Market (Overenskomst, for the reminder shortened to ALM) or at the individual firm level, often closely aligned to the ALM. Participation in unemployment insurance is voluntary, and while a highly regulated area, one that is also somewhat competitive. There is very limited protection against termination, typically only 3 months for positions held under 3 years and in only rare cases does termination periods exceed six months.

[1] The Danish active labor market policy is the most expensive in the world today. While economic reforms have been effective in increasing labor supply the active job placement effort, particularly the municipal-run Jobcentre, has been highly critiqued as ineffective and costly.

This structure dates back to the September Compromise of 1899 which created a constitution for the labor market. The compromise was a trade-off to secure profit for firms and security for workers. In 1960, the Basic Agreement revised the September Compromise, and cemented that labor relations should as much as possible be governed at both the general and local level on voluntary terms. In 1994 and 1996, the Social Democratic government initiated the active labor market policy in an attempt to combat a legacy of youth unemployment and to reform the labor market. This was de facto the birth of Flexicurity. In other words at the very tail-end of the twentieth century. The concept was "carrot and stick". When unemployed partook in activations schemes, actively sought employment, or signed up for further education, there were benefits, but if the citizen was obstinate, benefits could be reduced. In large part this took over from a norm-based system in the local chapters of unions under which motivation—or opportunity—challenged members was often personally sought out by the local chairman and put to work in firms needing workers, a system that had been declining since the 1970s introduction of Bistandsloven.

The voluntary unemployment insurance system (dagpenge) dates back to the 1907 Dagpengelov, other completely run government systems, like kontanthjælp (literally cash helping) also exist, but are less lucrative for the recipient. Dagpenge is a partly self-insured system of payments into insurrance pool (payment into which is tax deductable), with large support from the state. It replaced earlier systems of mutual insurance found in many unions. The law has been revised several times later, both in regards to who is eligible for benefits, the time period people can receive benefits and other terms. The state pays roughly 80% of the cost for individuals on the scheme, and the maximum amount is below many entry level jobs, causing many higher earners to buy additional insurance or to leave the scheme completely.

Another advantage of the Basic Agreement is that the incumbent government can call for special tripartite negotiations (trepartsforhandlinger) between the organizations of employers, employees, and the government. Such a scheme is useful to settle large societal reforms before these are put into law or if ALM negotiations have stranded. A famous example is the Conservative Prime Minister Poul Schlüter use of the scheme in 1987 to issue the "Commen Resolution", which paved the way for the labor market pensions that were later implemented in the following ALMs.

Challenges

The changing nature of the unions is putting pressure on the system. While the employers in Denmark often welcome collective bargaining due to the lower transaction cost resulting from an effective system, it is increasingly questionable how large a labor force the unions actually represent? Members are opting out or only joining the unemployment security (A-Kasse). The unions' response has largely been to attempt to force exclusivity agreements whereby workers must be organized in a particular union. Generally, the unions, besides having large organizations and many employees have been largely reactionary in their labor policies rather than playing an active role in envisioning the future post-industrial labor market and newer remuneration schemes like group-based performance pay. This strategy has likely let to the declining popularity and membership numbers. The still very close ties to the Social Democratic party are also a potential liability today.

A fundamental challenge to the system is the actual job market itself. When the model was envisioned there were few public sector job, whereas now the public sector has almost monopolized several sectors. The issue is that the model's strength; that it keeps transactions cost down and economic efficiency high relies on competition both among firms and among workers. There is no competition in these industries and hence the only possible option is to regulate based on different private industries. When public employees do not accept this outcome, trouble arises as the state de facto is negotiating with itself.

Due to the build-in wage balancing between the private sector and the public sector, the Danish model exposes the welfare state to Baumol disease.[2] Since the private sector is facing competition from global market exposure its efficiency is rising faster than the public sector, which also experiences some efficiency increase, but at a slower pace. When private sector efficiency increases, so do its wages. Wages are then regulated up in the public sector to match the private sector, and as a result the public sector becomes increasingly costly without a corresponding increase in efficiency, while being experienced as a continuously poorer offering by

[2] Baumol, *The Cost Disease*; Christoffersen, *Det mindst ringe: Om demokratiet i velfærdsstaten*; Karsten Bo Larsen, "Borgerlig liberal sundhedspolitik", In: Brian Degn Mårtensson, & Stefan Kirkegaard Sløk-Madsen (eds.), *Borger og Stat: en dansk indføring i liberale og konservative idéer* (Aarhus: Klim, 2022).

both workers and the public—despite it actually having seen improvements over time; just not matching the private sector or the increase in expenses from higher wages. It is akin to using a 20-year-old computer today—sure it is infinitely better than what was around 30 years ago, but it would still feel like a major setback compared to what you are used to now.

As mentioned above, there is no state-set minimum wage in Denmark, which cause some interesting challenges. Firstly, due to the free movement of labor within the EU, which demand that employers follow the laws, but not the ALMs, both trade unions and local firms worry about social dumping with imported labor from other member states. Another challenge is related to immigrations. While there is no minimum wage law, the de facto minimum wage—the equilibrium if you will—is likely around 130 DKK per hour for adults. The so-called integrationssydelser, a lower level of kontanthjælp, mainly aiming at non-western immigrants de facto places the hourly wage well below that, but as there are no jobs to get in the spread between that level and the 130-level, where these workers are often not competitive due to lacking language skills, social issues, etc., there is a de facto poverty trap for such individuals, particularly as the price levels are also set higher and even if job paid less, after tax it would not be feasible to take them.

As both employers and employees have historically been organized in their respective organization to a very high degree, the ALM have created the de facto general terms and condition of the Danish labor market—also for workers not officially hired under the agreement terms. All in all, the Danish model is favorable to businesses because it lowers, or rather socialize, transactions cost significantly.[3] Both in discovering and negotiating the price of labor, and in matters of termination costs. That said, it is not a cheap system and it relies on high and often progressive taxation.

[3] Ronald H. Coase, "The Nature of the Firm", *Economica*, 4:16 (1937), pp. 386–405; Kevin Carson, "Labor Struggle: A Free Market Model", *Center for a Stateless Society* (2015), https://c4ss.org/content/34897, Accessed Jan 27, 2021. Roderick T. Long, "Corporations Versus the Market, Or Whip Conflation Now", *CATO Unbound* (2008), https://www.cato-unbound.org/2008/11/10/roderick-t-long/corporations-versus-market-or-whip-conflation-now/, Accessed Jan 27, 2021.

The Cooperative Movement

In the Jutlandic village of Hjedding in 1882, a worldwide commercial business model innovation was born; the cooperative firm. In this specific case; a dairy. The idea was that all suppliers were co-owners. This meant that more people shared the burden of capital requirements—an early form of crowdfunding. The important emphasis being on heads, not wealth, when deciding among shareholders. But more importantly, it made even small farms more profitable by sharing revenue from shared production facilities. This in turn decreased the need for farmer families to take wage work off farms, and increased the spare time for schooling for kids. Prior to this business model, the agricultural industry was dominated by manors or other individually owned mills and diaries buying up the milk from farmers, which was both inefficient and less profitable.[4]

To make production of goods like butter profitable and industrialized, a large output of milk was needed. This was beyond the capabilities of the individual and often small farms. By joining forces new product innovations also materialized, most notably skimmed milk which was used for pig fodder creating the bacon that became an export miracle in the UK. The cooperative movement and particularly the innovations in both products and production that they birthed were in large part a key driver in explaining why Danish agriculture did in fact grow despite increasing globalized competition from the nineteenth century onwards. Path of the reason is also the supportive (almost mercantilist) government trade policy, particularly pre-1864, but to lesser degree also after, which favored dairy production and trade.[5]

The clear advantage of the cooperative model was the ability to produce industry-scale quality goods that were competitive both in terms of cost and price, while utilizing the dispersed family-firm-based agricultural value chain at the time. In the 1950s, the diaries consolidated into two rival companies Mejeriselskaberne Danmark and Kløver who after years of fierce competition and many price wars merged into MD Foods at the turn of the twentieth century and is now the global cooperative Arla Foods with an annual revenue of above 10 billion EUR. The cooperative

[4] Dybdahl et al., *Danmarks historie: De nye klasser 1870–1913.*

[5] I. Henriksen, M. Lampe, & P. Sharp, "The Strange Birth of Liberal Denmark: Danish Trade Protection and the Growth of the Dairy Industry Since the Mid-nineteenth Century 1", *The Economic History Review*, 65:2 (2012), pp. 770–788.

business model spread from it's 1882 birth and became the Cooperative Movement—Andelsbevægelsen.[6]

Often time, the trusting and homogeneous culture of rural Danish living is used to explain the popularity, rise, and commercial longevity of the cooperative firms. While such norms and informal institutions likely played a role, the cooperatives were not idealistic syndicates. Rather they made extensive use of monitoring, contacts and a willing supportive legal system—they were very much for-profit entities.[7]

An early example of the spread of the model was meat production in 1887, which had similar properties as milk production. Retail quickly followed and Forenede Danske Brugsforeninger (FDB) was founded in 1896 from an 1884 initiative from Zealand; Fællesforeningen for Danmarks Brugsforeninger. Today named Coop Danmark A/S. Coop is still the second largest retail player with a market share of 38%, a revenue of roughly 50 billion DKK, 1200 shops and 40,000 employees, and 1.8 million members, and even runs a banking division. Over the course of the twentieth century, FDB spread to other Nordic countries and launched several household and quintessential Danish brands, like Cirkel Kaffe (coffee).

The famous Danish design and architecture style known from such designers and artists as Poul Henningsen (1894–1967) and his famous lamp and the globally renowned Arne Jacobsen (1902–1971) similarly is interwoven with the cooperative movement which popularized their democratic Bauhaus style design principles. FDB Furniture was, for instance, founded in 1942 with a vision that furniture should provide space for humans. It had Børge Mogensen (1914–1972) as the first head of design and populated thousands of homes with quality design classics at relative affordable prices.

The first cooperative businesses grew largely out of the Gruntvignism, the folk high school movement, and the farmer party Venstre, and in fact the early economic success helped politically empower these ideas. However, the labor movement soon followed and established several of their own cooperative firms. One of the more famous ones was the brewery Stjernen (The Star) founded in 1902 in Frederiksberg.

[6] Fellman et al., *Creating Nordic Capitalism: The Business History of a Competitive Periphery*.

[7] I. Henriksen, M. Hviid, & P. Sharp, "Law and Peace: Contracts and the Success of the Danish Dairy Cooperatives", *The Journal of Economic History*, 72:1 (2012), pp. 197–224.

The philosophy was simple; if workers drink beer, they might as well drink their own. Founded by the Workers Bakery Cooperative (Arbejdernes Fællesbageri) and supported from unionized brewery works. While enjoying commercial success in the 1920 and 1930s, and despite producing some ground breaking and iconic marketing campaigns, the brewery shot down in 1964. A key issue for Stjernen and other worker cooperatives was their focus on employee rights—which made them popular places to work—rather than owner-profit. This made it hard to rationalize and compete with other types of firms (Fig. 6.1).

In the early twentieth century, the Danish state made several attempts to export the cooperative business model outside the Nordics, particularly to support related industries like farm machinery and education. These attempts met with little success and it is interesting to ask why? A potential explanation is that the same level of trust that enabled the welfare state, might also have enabled the cooperative movement. In Denmark, the model is still alive today and windmills and apartment buildings are often cooperatives, somewhat based on the same principles.

Fig. 6.1 Stjernen advertisement: Despite the socialist beginnings, Stjernen was not opposed to use individuals as spokespeople for their "star" brand. Here the superstar of the time Oswald Helmuth is saying: "A star likes to drink a star"

Industrial Foundation Ownership

Industrial foundations ownership[8] is at heart a tax scheme that existed until 1987 and meant that shares in a company can be permanently transferred free of tax to a foundation. Foundation creation still has tax advantages to this day and remains a popular ownership structure in Denmark. This foundation will then pay out dividends according to a charter. This typically involves some specifications of recipients, like the founders' family, but also a social aim like charities or helping the less fortunate. As such, they fill an important hole in the welfare state model, that of private giving. Maybe due to the high tax rate private philanthropy and charity is not common in Denmark, but the foundations give out significant amounts—18 billion DKK in 2018.[9] Who should receive is decided by board of trustees according to the foundation charter. The board of trustees can be completely different from, or a mix of the underlying companys board members. In average, however trustees are 10 years senior to regular board members, perhaps due to the more charitable nature of the work—they are also on average paid less. When a foundation is set up, the Foundation Authority must approve of the charter, and they also audit the existing foundations, but cannot impact the commercial decisions.

Foundation ownership is not a uniquely Danish institution, but Denmark is unique in how prevalent it is. A. P. Møller Mærsk, Carlsberg, and Novo Nordisk are the largest Danish companies and under industrial foundation ownership. The footprint of the ownership is significant, as shown in Fig. 6.2.

What is more, the foundations owned firms are quite successful. Surprisingly so. A study of 300 largest non-financial foundations owned versus investor owned and family owned firms found that in the period 1982–1992 no significant difference in sales growth or accounting returns (ROE, ROA). Further, foundation-owned companies show higher profit margins and lower asset turnover both to a significant degree in the period

[8] This section is largely based on Steen Thomsen, "Foundation Ownership and Firm Performance: A Review of the International Evidence", *Corporate Governance in Contention* (2018), pp. 66–85; Henry Hansmann & Steen Thomsen, "The Governance of Foundation-Owned Firms", *The Journal of Legal Analysis*, 13:1 (2021), pp. 172–230.

[9] Incidentally most other charity, particularly to sport and youth activities, is given out from the profit of the state-owned betting company *Danske Spil* contribution south of 3 billion DKK yearly.

Contribution to total employment	5%
Annual value addition	10%
Contribution to total R&D	50%
Share of stock market Capitalization	70%

Fig. 6.2 The Industrial foundation footprint on Danish Economy (*Source* Thomsen, "Foundation Ownership and Firm Performance: A Review of the International Evidence")

and seem to be more conservatively managed by having higher solvency (equity/assets) and lower earnings volatility (standard deviation of return on equity).[10] At the end of the twentieth century Thomsen and Rose examined foundation-owned listed companies and found them to be as efficient as other companies when looking at risk-adjusted stock returns, accounting returns, and firm value (Tobin's Q). They are different in other ways too; foundation-owned companies replace board members and managers less often. They are more research-intensive. They survive longer with more stable earnings and less leveraged balance sheets.[11] They grow slower, but with more stable growth.[12]

What is worth pondering is why they perform so well, as corporate governance theory would suggest otherwise: they are less profit-oriented and therefore might be less willing to cut costs, and they might be reluctant to seek outside equity or engage in M&A. On the plus side they appear to be attractive long-term places of employment with above average remuneration and below average employee churn.[13]

As Thomsen states "*According to what is known as 'the theory of the firm' in economics, there are a number of reasons why foundation-owned*

[10] Steen Thomsen, "Foundation Ownership and Economic Performance", *Corporate Governance: An International Review*, 4:4 (1996), pp. 212–221.

[11] Steen Thomsen, Thomas Poulsen, Christa Børsting, & Johan Kuhn, "Industrial Foundations as Long-Term Owners", *Corporate Governance: An International Review*, 26:3 (2018), pp. 180–196.

[12] Christa Børsting, Johan Kuhn, Thomas Poulsen, & Steen Thomsen, "The Performance of Danish Foundation-owned Companies", *Unpublished Working Paper, The Research Project on Industrial Foundations* (2014).

[13] Christa Børsting, & Steen Thomsen, "Foundation Ownership, Reputation, & Labour", *Oxford Review of Economic Policy*, 33:2 (2017), pp. 317–338.

firms should fail, or at least underperform. They lack the profit incentive extolled in economics since Adam Smith. They are insulated from the market for corporate control, and are limited in their ability to diversify risk, as recommended in corporate finance. Foundation boards lack the accountability emphasized in political science and management theory, since they refer essentially to no one but themselves".[14] It is however worth remembering that all ownership structures have their drawbacks

- Traded ownership either publicly or by private equity is high financialized.
- Family business face succession concerns which can be impacted family feuds, or nepotism.
- State-owned enterprises have soft budget constraints and suffer from direct and indirect political interference and insecurity.

What might be the saving grace for foundations might be the distinctive Danish context. High taxes limit monetary reward, which could relatively increase other types of benefits for trustees. The country is small and tightknit where reputation matters, and the integral part in philanthropy that foundations are expected to play might also create the same sense of urgency as expected from the profit motive, as experiments show that people show less moral hazard when working for charity as opposed to personal consumption.[15] It might also be that trustees identify with the success and purpose of the charter as argued in identity economics.[16] So again here, we might see the importance of trust and low corruption rates.

[14] Thomsen, "Foundation Ownership and Firm Performance: A Review of the International Evidence".

[15] Oege Dijk & Martin Holmén, "Charity, Incentives, and Performance", *Journal of Behavioral and Experimental Economics*, 66 (2017), pp. 119–128.

[16] George A. Akerlof, & Rachel E. Kranton, *Identity Economics How Our Identities Shape Our Work, Wages, and Well-Being* (Princeton: Princeton University Press, 2010); Roland Bénabou, & Jean Tirole, "Identity, Morals, and Taboos: Beliefs as Assets", *The Quarterly Journal of Economics*, 126:2 (2011), pp. 805–855. Roland Bénabou, & Jean Tirole, *Laws and Norms* (Cambridge, MA: National Bureau of Economic Research, 2011). In psychology, effects like these are labeled "organizational identification", see Blake E. Ashforth, Spencer H. Harrison, & Kevin G. Corley, "Identification in Organizations: An Examination of Four Fundamental Questions", *Journal of Management*, 34:4 (2008), pp. 325–374.

Købmandskab: A Danish Approach to Selling?

When driving around the Danish countryside in the summer, there are often booths with produce for sale or small yard sales. Such commercial initiatives are often advertised with a Dannebrog; Selling and nationhood are linked in Denmark.[17] This is little wonder, as Denmark has always been a maritime nation, but it has also always been a commercial nation, not least fueled by a lack of national resources and a unique geography. We have evidence of the immense importance of trade going back to 13,000 BC,[18] where the eruption of the Laacher See volcano cut off trade, and resulted in a societal decline. Later, historically speaking we see trade networks connecting Denmark and Egypt.[19] The famous Vikings were also likely as much tradesmen as they were plunderers and warriors. While Denmark hence was more or less considered barbarian untill around year 1000 the complexities of trade was not missing, albeit in a slightly different take. This is to some extent reflected in the language. In Danish the word for "buy" is "køb". The Danish traditional word for a sales person or business man is "købmand" or "buying man". Note; it is not "selling man". One explanation could be that a business man buys low and sells high, but seeing as the word is also used to describe local grocery shops, it could also be that the word describes market exchange as being inherently customer-centric. A "købmand" is where you go to buy what you cannot produce yourself. Trade for what you do not have, which is why trade flourished in the Bronze Age as that required foreign resources, but declined in the Iron Age, as Iron can be produced locally. Figure 6.3 shows a language study of European languages and we see that in ~33% of the surveyed European languages the relation seems to exist where commercialization is not selling to consumers, but consumers buying from a vendor. This is in stark contrast to the modern English word of "merchant" which comes from the Latin "*mercari*" which means to trade and has an inherent relation to negotiation. Interestingly in Old English and Scottish we do see the connection too (which is why Britain is marked separately in Fig. 6.3).

[17] Ronit, "Handelens vej er altid kulturens vej, Det Danske Handelskammer 1742–1992".

[18] Riede, "Da himlen faldt ned".

[19] Jeanette V*arberg*, Flemming *Kaul, & Bernard Gratuze*, "Glasvejen", *Skalk*, 6 (2014).

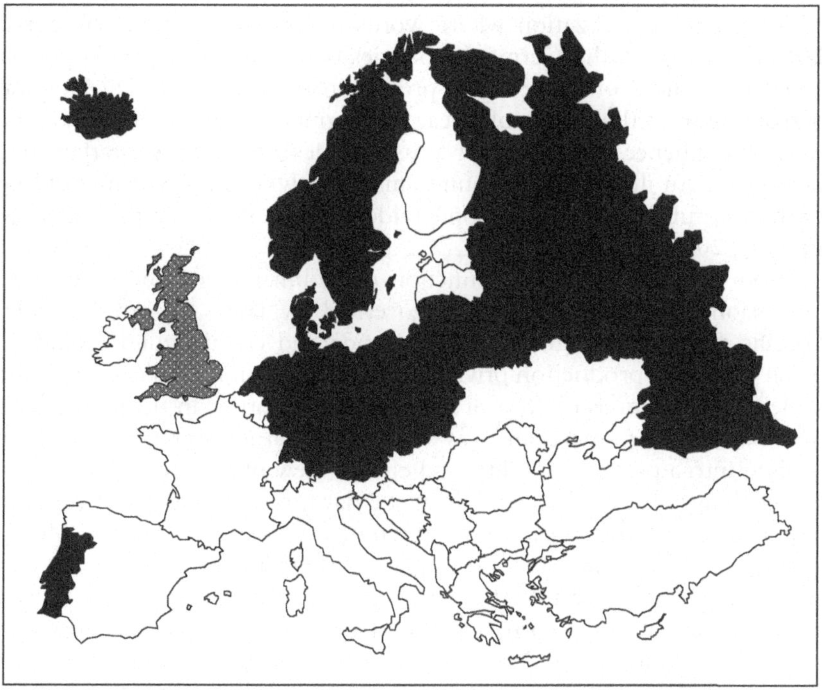

Fig. 6.3 Sales as a profession or a function (*Note* Portugal does not fit the analysis in the text. However as Portuguese develop as a distinct language after the Roman occupation in was heavily influenced by concurring Germanic tribes at the time. Old Irish and Welsh was heavily influenced by Latin and Rome, and likely therefore also lack the connection. *Source* Own analysis)

Hayek describes languages as spontaneous orders that emerge to support human activity and organization.[20] As such languages reflect the society that formed them and found them useful. We can probably never truly know why words formed like they did, but looking again at Fig. 6.3, we see the "buy" connection in mainly Germanic languages, but less so in Latin ones. One theory could be that Latin society quickly evolved

[20] Friedrich August von Hayek, *The Constitution of Liberty* (Chicago: University of Chicago Press, 2011); S. Egashira, 2017. "Hayek, Evolution, and Imanishi", In: Robert Leeson (Ed.), *Hayek: A Collaborative Biography* (Houndmills, Basingstoke, Hampshire: Palgrave Macmillan, 2013), pp. 435–454.

to a level of specialization where words describe professions (Roberts, 2011), whereas in the Germanic societies of a 1000 years past, a person could rarely hold one specialized profession for a longer time. A typical person might in the course of a year be a farmer, a trader, a hunter, and a warrior and hence the language was used to describe *functions* rather than *professions*. An illustration is found among early Vikings which could be both peaceful traders and fearsome raiders on the *same* voyage (Bately & Englert, 2007).

From the year 1000, the function of Købmand does become more professionalized and increasingly governed by laws and royal decree. Specific towns where given rights to trade and certain guilds could be given trade and production privileges. As such Denmark reflect much the same development as the rest of north Western Europe in the period, and just like elsewhere merchant was a sort of social leftover from a society devised into a peasant, nobility, and church view of society.

Yet things change fairly rapidly at the dawn of the nineteenth century. Coinciding with the spread of enlightenment ideas in Denmark a cultural change of large significance took place. Where in the recent past, and still in much of the rest of the world, commercial activities were viewed with a certain level of scorn, and was at most a means to other forms of social advancement—an idea dating back to Aristotle's.[21] Now it became desirable in Denmark to want to work commercially for its own sake.[22]

Several large changes further impacted the role of the merchant class and approaches to commerce and business in the nineteenth century, many of which are described in the biographical study of the local Samsø merchant and entrepreneur Lars Rasmussen (1817–1899).[23] Particularly his need to adapt his business model to the changing times of more professional agricultural sector, an increasingly modern state apparatus and the ever more global market. Lars Rasmussen settled in Samsø as

[21] Aristotle, *Politics* (Chicago: University of Chicago Press, 2013); Scott Meikle, "Aristotle on Business", *The Classical Quarterly*, 46:1 (1996), pp. 138–151.

[22] Flemming Mikkelsen, "Industrielle foretagere i Odense omkring 1870", *Erhvervshistorisk Årbog* (1980); Ole Markussen, "Dansk industrihistorie – præsentation af et forskningsområde", *Fortid og Nutid*, 32:2 (1985), pp. 79–99.

[23] Søren Bitsch Christensen, "Menneske først, købmand så? Et biografisk studie i samspillet mellem optegnelsesbøger, økonomisk modernisering, livsformer og samvirkebevægelser i 1800-tallet - købmand Lars Rasmussen på Samsø", *Fortid og Nutid*, 2 (2000), pp. 91–123.

it was a shortcut to establish a business there as it was not a town with trade privileges (which require him to have citizen status), but also exempt from the legal constrains normally placed on rural areas regrading trade and commercial affairs. A sort of unplanned Economic Free Zone of the time.

In the detailed description of his business, it is interesting to note a couple of things. People of all classes often brought on credit and the local grocer was de facto a financial institution, at least in providing more mediums of exchange and even credit lines. Lars Rasmussen himself was further part of a larger network of credit giving among merchants, traders and the bourgeoning industrialists. This financial aspect of the business was not commercially pursued for interest income or other financial income, but rather simply to facilitate more trade. That it could work is a testament to the large trust existing in the population already at that time. The clear downside was however extreme exposure to general economic trends to the point where it can be argued that retail particularly, but most business really, at the time was a form of derived demand in terms of risk profile.[24] Hence, both trust and societal exposure was part of shaping the Danish view of selling at the beginning of the twentieth century.

Another aspect was tolerance. Both Adam Smith and Voltaire highlighted tolerance as a moral virtue of commercial culture. This is also highlighted in the role of local Danish merchants and retailers. While hierarchy and social difference certainly existed, one place to meet across social divides—particularly in local communities—was when engaging in market activities. This likely contributed further to build community and trust in the populace.

We also see an early modern professionalization of the commercial profession spearheaded by business philanthropy and later supported and ultimately largely taken over by the state; business education.[25] The process starts when the businessman Niels Brock (1731–1802) dies childless in 1802. A part of his inheritance was giving to what is now The Danish Chamber of Commerce (Dansk Erhverv) with the purpose of establishing a Danish business school on the model of the one he attended

[24] Alfred Marshall, *Principles of Economics* (London: Palgrave Macmillan UK, 2013).

[25] Ronit, "Handelens vej er altid kulturens vej, Det Danske Handelskammer 1742–1992".

in Lubeck in his youth. It would take some years to make good on the obligation, and only after the establishment of an agricultural university (now part University of Copenhagen) and a polytechnic institution (now the Technical University of Denmark). What is today known as Niels Brock Business College Copenhagen was founded in 1881. The Danish Society for Education and Business expanded higher business education further and in 1917 founded what would become Copenhagen Business School—today one of the most prestigious business schools and social science universities. Today both institutions are run by the state.

Of the original people involved in the establishment of Danish business education was particularly the newer younger breed of prominent Copenhagen business elites, such as etatsråd Harald Fritsche (1833–1905) and head of the national bank Moritz Levy (1824–1892). Besides education, the emphasis was on helping young business people go abroad to get experience and knowledge. What is also evident from their writings is that they saw "modern" business as different from the merchants of old. According to them, success in the past was only possible if you already had access to large amounts of capital and was ultimately lucky. Modern business in their view was different. It was a path of social and material improvement open to all who was willing to work hard, and success came not from luck, but from knowledge utilization. The links to the ideas of Deirdre McCloskey and Poul Romer are clear. On the academic side, politician and businessman C. Hage (1848–1930) published the first edition of his Handbook in Commercial Science in 1892 with a foreword by C. F. Tietgen—himself coming from meager beginnings in Odense like a commercial H. C. Andersen.[26] The book is a 1200 plus page brick which saw many subsequent edition in the twentieth century and it concerns all matters of commercial life, organization, legal and related topics and was meant as "a study for the young, and a useful tool for the older".[27]

Moving into the twentieth century our knowledge of Danish sales is unfortunately underresearched. As discussed in Chapter 5, we know of high stakes cases of top hat wearing cigar smoking dealers in high

[26] Ole Lange, *Stormogulen: C.F. Tietgen - en finansmand, hans imperium og hans tid 1829–1901* (Copenhagen: Gyldendal, 2006).

[27] Christopher Hage, *Haandbog I Handelsvidenskab* (Copenhagen, 1894); Jørgen Hansen, Niels Kærgård, & Jens Thomsen, *Med hånden på statskassen: Økonomer i regering* (Copenhagen: DJØF Forlag, 2019).

capitalism, but precious little is known about the smaller companies' approaches. We know that the Danish shipping industry quickly gained a global reputation as good sales people.[28] Moving to the innovative companies of post-World War II fame it seems highly likely that sales played a significant role in explaining their success. Yet, we know very little about how they did it, and if it differed from other nations. Sales in many ways remain a blackbox for many researchers and historians. Was Danish commercial success linked to a method or was it external factors like geography or politics that cleared the way? Were the Danish products just in high demand? All this is interesting to study further. One example is found in Lars Larsen (1948–2019)—the founder of JYSK A/S[29] a magnificent retail success of the late twentieth century. He greatly emphasized sales and was quick to innovate here—He was, for instance, among the first to use TV commercials in Denmark. Appearing on screen in person with the words; "I was a great offer for you", in a trusting lowkey Jutland accent. Today a legendary Danish pop culture reference.[30]

Institutionalized Daycare

One of the main changes in the twentieth century was institutionalized daycare. In 2000, almost 100% of 4 year olds were in public daycare institutions.[31] Childcare went from being a family matter undertaken by the wife or elderly relatives with private market solutions being limited and only for the very wealthy or for socially marginalized children like orphans in 1900. The first step to mass childcare was the child asylums which started around 1900 to grow as a sector due to the increased urbanization and industrialization to around 100 in total. Such child asylums were often driven by voluntary efforts and by bourgeoisie women and often centered around religious or social convictions, with often several hundred children associated and very strict discipline and little to no focus

[28] Chris Jephson, & Henning Morgen, *Oprettelse af globale muligheder: Maersk Line i containerisering 1973–2013* (Copenhagen: Gyldendal: 2014).

[29] Lars Larsen had in 2004 his autobiography (see note below) distributed to all households in part to teach the joy and merits of selling.

[30] Lars Larsen, *Go'daw jeg hedder Lars Larsen: - jeg har et godt tilbud: en selvbiografi* (Aarhus: Hansen Mejlgade, 2004).

[31] Det Økonomiske Råd, "Kapitel III - Dynamiske effekter af offentlige udgifter", In: *Dansk Økonomi, Forår 2017* (2017).

on child development. Some firms also established daycare facilities if they relied on a female workforce.

The next development was driven by people inspired by Fröbelian ideas such as the sisters Anna and Bertha Wullf (1878–1875) and the couple Hedevig (1842–1926) and Sophus Bagger (1848–1942). They created the first attempts at modern kindergardens with state funds. This developed to a general state grand to kindergardens in 1919, and from the 20's it became common and not considered socially stigmatized to send children to daycare facilities. The Social Democratic movement embraced in the concept, and along with public schools pushed for their spread, use, and importance. It was almost a social calling, like stopping for red lights and paying taxes, to institutionalize your offspring as early and as much as possible. In no small way pushed by many feminists at the time. Kindergardens as a tool to fight social ills and poor life outcomes became sanctified in the social reform of 1933 and their number grew steadily till the beginning of the 1970s. A true explosion came in the 1960s where the number of women joining the workforce grew similarly. Daycare institutions further got a separate law code in 1964. As part of the bistandlov in 1976 the municipalities took over operations of the daycare facilities, which quickly became a mayor budget point and political issues in local elections. In 1993 Social Democratic Prime Minister Poul Nyrup Rasmussen put the screws on further by requiring municipalities to offer a guarantee of childcare service.

The obvious benefit of large daycare usage is that more people, in particular women have been given the opportunity to pursue active labor participation in the twentieth century. Another benefit is that child participation in institutionalized daycare seems positively correlated with grade point average in the final year of public school,[32] however the control group is not home caring, but rather the option of dagpleje, where a private person takes care of a smaller group of kids for pay. Recent research also shows that the effect on life outcome does suffer from marginal returns, where increased investment above the current average does not yield significant improvements, in other words the dynamic effects of public spending have a cut-off point here at least.[33]

[32] Nabanita Datta Gupta, Marianne Simonsen, "Academic Performance and Type of Early Childhood Care", *Economics of Education Review*, 53 (2016), pp. 217–229.

[33] Det Økonomiske Råd, "Kapitel IV: Tidlig Indsats", In: *Dansk Økonomi Forår 2021* (2021).

While the immense popularity of institutionalized daycare can look like a success, recently several points of critiques has been mounted. Firstly, from parents, who perhaps fueled by a guilty conscience, demands that more and more resources are spent on the daycare sector, despite a dwindling talent pool and clear diminishing returns. The sector itself likely also suffers from effects of Baumol's disease as discussed earlier. Further, the near monopoly held by the municipalities is likely hurtful for organizational learning, innovation, and efficiency. The sector is also very rigidly governed in terms of management digression and employee remuneration options.

That said, the many special interest, such as unions, hold on to the model and are very harsh defenders of the merits of institutionalized daycare. In fact, parents also have very little choice, as most families in Denmark are dependent on a dual income and the tax system to a far degree punishes parents who wish to take care of their kids themselves.[34]

Finally, there is the issue of health concerns. Kids in daycare spread diseases and germs rapidly—which might have both positive and negative long-term health effects. However, at the end of the twentieth century, children in daycare were home sick between 3–8% of the days the institutions were open. Surprisingly, the effect of this on the parents' health and productivity has never been analyzed.[35]

Extensive Pension System

Saving for old age is inherently hard. It is not that people do not have preferences for a nice retirement. Rather they display myopic behavior and put off saving. For instance, a classic insight from behavioral economics, shows that whether people have to opt in or opt out of pension saving schemes matter greatly for their usage.[36] The problem is also increasingly significant by the simple fact that most people live longer. Danes born

[34] Sørensen, *Moderland: når staten kupper børnene.*

[35] Birgitte Gade Koefoed, Anne Margrethe Nielsen, & Lis M. Keiding, "The Impact of Selected Environmental Factors on the Morbidity of Children in Day Care Centers", *Ugeskrift for læger*, 164:49 (2002), pp. 5759–5764.

[36] Shlomo Benartzi & Richard H. Thaler, "Behavioral Economics and the Retirement Savings Crisis", *Science*, 339:6124 (2013), pp. 1152–1153; Rajiv Prabhakar, "Why Do People Opt-Out or Not Opt-Out of Automatic Enrolment? A Focus Group Study of Automatic Enrolment into a Workplace Pension in the United Kingdom", *Journal of European Social Policy*, 27:5 (2017), pp. 447–457; Heinz P. Rudolph, "Pension Funds

in 1950 could expect to live to around 72, already immensely improved from 52 in 1900. In other words, my father's life expectancy at birth is my retirement age. People born at the turn of the twentieth century was fast closing in on 90 in average, and what is more is the health conditions of the average 70 year old is markedly different and continuously improving.[37]

Denmark has—as most welfare states—a long tradition for bookmarked pension schemes. Schemes where the pension is related to the past labor market participation type and rate. The earliest scheme was for state-employed civil servants and date from 1849. At first, the pension was only for royal appointees but was by 1872 expanded to those appointed by the ministers. It was generous schemes aimed at creating loyalty to the state and attracting talent. New, and significantly larger, groups containing teachers, police officers, postal workers and others, got a pension scheme in 1919 with the Civil Service Act (Tjenestemandsloven). Here again the desire was to create life-long employment in the public sector, which would be rewarded in old age. The level of pensions set a benchmark that other segments of the labor force would measure against for the majority of the twentieth century.

While private market pension schemes were rare, they did exist and already around the 1870s several firms in the financial sector established pension schemes. This was considered smart, as it aligned individual risk profiles with the long-term survival and performance of the financial firm. In 1917 employers and employees created Pensionsforsikringsanstalten (today known as PFA). The idea here was to remove the ties to the individual firm, where employees could lose their pension if it went bankrupt, or indeed it could go bankrupt from pension obligations. As Scandinavian Airlines came close to late in the 20th century, and several times since. It also increased mobility in the labor force where employees could change employment without fearing for their pension rights. We see here a clear different motivation than for the public pension schemes which aimed at stability rather than employee dynamics in the private sector.

The demand for pension schemes grew rapidly after the Second World War and particularly in the 1960–1970 the number of both pension savers

with Automatic Enrollment Schemes: Lessons for Emerging Economies", *World Bank Policy Research Working Paper*, no. 8726 (2019).

[37] Folketinget - Sundhedsudvalget og Det Politisk-Økonomiske Udvalg Økonomigruppen, *3. Udvalgssekretariat* (October 18, 2006).

and scheme providers exploded. While the period still saw schemes based on promises of payment at retirement, the market increasingly moved toward general insurance where payout was not based on employment relation but on what was paid in.[38]

Besides the individual labor market pension schemes, Denmark also has the peoples pension and ATP (Bookmarked Additive Pension), which has an element of redistribution between recipients. The People Pension was established in 1956 and despite the growing interest in private pension schemes was still the only pension for approximately 2/3 of the labor force in 1960. This led to inequality in old age, and parliament tried to amend this with ATP in 1964. This scheme paid out a similar payment to all labor market participants between 18 and 66 year of age. It was financed 1/3 from employees and 2/3 from employers and centrally managed. It was designed so that the pension addition to the individual recipient was dependent on how many years they worked, not on the size of the salary, which made the scheme particularly important for individuals without private saving schemes. ATP would grow to be among the largest Danish investment sources.

Inequality with regards to pension remained a hot political issue up untill the 1980s. The Confederation of Labor Unions (LO) suggested a reform in 1985. They wanted the state to play a larger role in pension schemes. The conservative-liberal government, and in time also the employer organizations—agreed that more people should join pension schemes, but disagreed on the role of the state. However, more private pension saving would remove fiscal pressure from the state pension payments, which was a tax financed "pay-as-you-go" system and a dangerous (future) drain on public resources. It was also a tool to help ease the economic dead water of the period. Instead of pay raises employees could get pension schemes, which would help ease inflation, and funds would be channeled from consumer spending to business investments.

The parties however disagreed on implementation. The unions wanted laws to mandate pensions and were not keen on demanding lower current wage increases. The parties further disagreed on how to administer payments. The unions wanted to control a common investment fund. This was something the employers feared gravely, as this would make

[38] Due-Nielsen, "Paul Hammerich: En danmarkskrønike 1945–72: Velfærd på afbetaling".

the unions immensely powerful investors and potentially give them large degree of control over many firms.

As the end of 1987 loomed, Denmark was in stagflation, mounting unemployment and a deficit on the payment balance. Against this background the conservative-liberal government initiated tripartite negations in November on a new model for pensions, the employer side was represented by Confederations of Danish Employers (DA) and Sammenslutningen af Landbrugets Arbejdsgiverorganisationer (SALA), with employees being represented by LO, and Fællesrådet for Danske Tjenestemands-og Funktionærorganisationer (FTF).

Already on December 8 a Common Resolution was signed which aimed to extend labor market pensions to all employees, but only in a way that would not harm the competitive situation of Danish businesses. This last element is important to note, because the unions here understood that first and foremost the rising unemployment had to be solved by (global) market forces.

This is an important step in Danish Capitalism, because the 100-year-old labor market struggle was reigned in. The unions acknowledged that labor demands had to be responsible and modest to allow for improved competitive power of the employers in a global marketplace. Worker demands was secondary to business results. Concretely, pay demands should aim to match countries where Danish firms were in direct competition, in the words of LO-president Finn Thorgrimson (1935–2019); "We prefer a jobparty, to a wageparty". This in turn could create a growing competitive labor market which would reward high performers, while not pushing out less capable workers.

While support from the government became lackluster, the market players took up the gauntlet themselves and made good on the common resolution in the following years and negotiations. Several of the new pension funds which were created as a result was owned jointly by employee and employer organizations. As of the year 2000, labor market pensions were extended to basically the whole organized labor market—even spreading to schemes for the self-employed. Today, many people have more spending power and even higher income as pensioners than they had doing their job life.

The Danish approach to pensions is important to appreciate. In it, we find the ultimate compromise in the labor struggle described by Marx; the bourgeois retains property and the right to organize production, while the proletariat get a stake in their "surplus value"—over time turning them into capitalist themselves (old Karl Marx would likely truly have hated that part). It also shows the power of market incentives. It created wealth, both to be used for investments, but also for millions of regular citizens who became more secure and able to adopt to changing opportunities. It also increased equality. It is in other words a huge success of twentieth century Danish Capitalism. However, ideologically speaking it is an odd child and trouble seems to be on the horizon which questions the longevity of the institution.

Ideologically speaking, forcing people to save up money is an attack on their personal freedom. The liberal party, Venstre, which together with three other parties comprised the ruling government 1987 was therefore also skeptical of the common agreement. The ideological issue becomes increasingly forefront when other investment classes are more lucrative, such as urban real estate. A large part of the success of forced saving has been fueled by the good international growth rates. In the twenty-first century growth has generally fallen, especially in Denmark, and both low to negative interest rates and looming inflations make safe good returns rarer. These are dangerous concerns for the Danish pension institutions which is a vanguard of market stability and an immensely important investment engine for Danish Capitalism.

Conclusion

This chapter attempted to highlight and present some dominant methods and institutions of Twentieth Century capitalism in Denmark. Some were planned, most emerged. Many aspects of the topics presented here are often misunderstood, like the voluntary market nature of the Danish labor market model.

A joint conclusion is that the successful Danish institutions are build-on, and often extended trust. But as the bureaucracy took over trust levels have been threatened and something to be vary of in the future. It is interesting that so many Danes willingly hand over their kids to strangers employed by a system for so many hours of their childhood. This certainly proves extended trust in both the system and your fellow citizens. This is also why, as the Baumol disease puts pressure on the relative productiveness of state produced welfare and trust—the number of parents seeking private schools has likely never been higher.

Trust and profit might be more linked than has been assumed in twentieth century Denmark. As exemplified with the cooperative model, profit is a residual of efficiency and provides safety against bad times, and the possibility of reinvestment—including in social causes. Consumers trust companies that provide quality (innovative) products and who become solid from their profit. Such consumer agency in a market is lacking when dealing with the state.

Finally, we see the mirror of the Danish struggle and balancing act between stability—the state—and dynamics—the market—played out in these institutions. The lesson from the Common Resolution is very noteworthy, and learned by market participants; each market participant has a role to play, and it is preferable to let the market solve disputes, and only use the blunt force of government intervention in the most dire situation, which participants also wants to avoid. This is in many ways a uniquely Danish outcome of the class struggle that engulfed the twentieth century. However, as I will comment on the last chapter, a lesson learned by market participants is hard to uphold if the voting majority are public servants.

CHAPTER 7

Danish Capitalism in the Twenty-First Century: Legacy and Changes in the First Two Decades

The State of the Kingdom in 2021

In this chapter, I will review what the immediate outcome of the twentieth century capitalism was in Denmark. Including some reasons and theorize on the causal relations. According to Tulluck the role of economic analysis is to disregard intentions and look at consequences, which is what I will attempt.[1] While business history is typically a bottom-up approach, this chapter is—due to the vastness of the subject matter—more top down. Also, I largely ignore COVID-19, both in terms of policy considerations and economic effects, since it is far too early to judge this in a historical light. Although I will comment shortly on some issues relating to the political response to the pandemic in the end.

In many ways, Danish Capitalism was a success in the twentieth century. Already since the early 2000's Denmark has been in or around the top ten most competitive economies.[2] As of 2019, Denmark is the 6th richest country among the 37 OECD countries. This GDP per capita

[1] Gordon Tullock, "The Welfare Costs of Tariffs, Monopolies, and Theft", *Economic Inquiry*, 5:3 (1967), pp. 224–232; Arthur Seldon, Gordon L. Brady, & Gordon Tullock, *Government Failure: A Primer in Public Choice* (Washington, DC: Cato Institute, 2002).

[2] World Economic Forum, *Global Competitiveness Report Special Edition 2020: How Countries are Performing on the Road to Recovery* (2020).

© The Author(s), under exclusive license to Springer Nature Switzerland AG 2022

S. K. Sløk-Madsen, *Danish Capitalism in the 20th Century*, Palgrave Studies in Economic History,
https://doi.org/10.1007/978-3-031-04267-6_7

result is largely driven by a high productivity (GDP per working hour), unfortunately the work effort is among the lowest in OECD countries (hours worked per capita), as shown in Fig. 7.1. A likely reason for the lower work effort could well be taxes, a policy sickness of the last quarter of the twentieth century. Denmark has had the highest tax revenue per GDP, since 2002, expect for 2017–2018, where France held the number one spot—shown in Fig. 7.1.[3] Despite some twenty-first century scandals and troublesome IT implementation, the Danish Tax Authority is extremely efficient, prompting some business owners to comment that there is no income tax, rather there is a tax on employing people, as income tax payments are for the majority part handled by the employer. This has led to speculations that Danes care less about taxes because they simply do not realize how much they are paying. Total tax pressure (tax and tariffs divided by GDP) is shown in Fig. 7.3 (Fig. 7.2).

The tax revenues, who are mainly paid by labor and consumption taxes like VAT (25% on most goods), and not corporate taxes, are used to fund public spending which amounted to 49,8% of GDP in 2019. Public expenditures were 24.1% of GDP. The issue of crumbling public debt from the expansive welfare state has been curtailed and today net public debt is well managed. In fact, the public sector is overfunded—public surplus in 2019 was 3.8% of GDP, largest among EU countries.

The country has—like many other Western states—seen an increase in legal regulation,[4] but managed to lighten the regulatory load and restraints on some key economic areas in the first decade of the twenty-first century, particularly the ease of starting and doing business, but also the loathed Lukkelov (retail closing law), which improved business opportunities for retail and consumer welfare alike.

Besides immigration and climate change, inequality has been among the hottest economic topics for politicians in the twenty-first century. To illustrate, in 2005, the then minister of Social affairs—Eva Kjer Hansen (b. 1964) in the liberal-conservative Fogh government had to withdraw and almost put the whole coalition in danger when she stated the fact that a dynamic market was more important than equality as a policy goals for prosperity. While all prime ministers since the Conservative

[3] See note 51.

[4] Jonas Herby, "Regelstaten", In Brian Degn Mårtensson, & Stefan Kirkegaard Sløk-Madsen (eds.), *Borger og Stat: en dansk indføring i liberale og konservative idéer* (Aarhus: Klim, 2022).

BNP per capita, US dollars			= GDP per hour worked, US dollars			x Working hours per capita		
1	Luxembourg	124.269	1	Ireland	112,7	1	Luxembourg	1127
2	Ireland	92.232	2	Luxembourg	110,3	2	South Korea	1030
3	Switzerland	73.969	3	Norway	96	3	New Zealand	942
4	Norway	70.382	4	Denmark	87,1	4	Mexico	934
5	USA	65.240	5	Belgium	80,9	5	Switzerland	925
6	Denmark	62.106	6	Switzerland	80	6	Czech Republic	908
7	Iceland	61.344	7	France	79,5	7	Japan	903
8	Holland	61.242	8	Austria	78,7	8	Israel	895
9	Austria	60.414	9	Sweden	78,3	9	Canada	875
10	Germany	57.558	10	Holland	77	10	Australia	866
11	Sweden	56.701	11	USA	77	11	Chile	855
12	Belgium	54.330	12	Germany	76,4	12	Estonia	849
13	Australia	54.263	13	Iceland	73,8	13	USA	847
14	Finland	53.160	14	Finland	71,4	14	Hungary	832
15	Canada	51.107	15	United Kingdom	66,1	15	Iceland	831
16	France	50.693	16	Italy	63,1	16	Greece	830
17	United Kingdom	49.912	17	Australia	62,7	17	Portugal	828
18	Italy	45.691	18	Spain	59,9	18	Ireland	818
19	New Zealand	45.163	19	Canada	58,4	19	Lithuania	812
20	Czech Republic	44.299	20	Slovenia	52,9	20	Slovenia	802
21	South Korea	43.678	21	Lithuania	49,2	21	Holland	795
22	Japan	43.643	22	Czech Republic	48,8	22	Latvia	780
23	Spain	43.471	23	Japan	48,4	23	Poland	770
24	Slovenia	42.409	24	New Zealand	48	24	Austria	767
25	Israel	41.463	25	Estonia	47,1	25	Slovakia	759
26	Estonia	40.040	26	Israel	46,3	26	United Kingdom	755
27	Lithuania	39.912	27	Portugal	45,7	27	Germany	753
28	Portugal	37.856	28	Turkey	45,6	28	Finland	745
29	Hungary	34.962	29	Poland	45,2	29	Norway	733
30	Poland	34.781	30	Slovakia	44,2	30	Spain	726
31	Slovakia	33.521	31	South Korea	42,4	31	Italy	725
32	Latvia	33.014	32	Latvia	42,3	32	Sweden	724
33	Greece	31.790	33	Hungary	42	33	Denmark	713
34	Turkey	28.423	34	Greece	38,3	34	Belgium	671
35	Chile	26.880	35	Chile	31,4	35	France	638
36	Mexico	21.244	36	Mexico	22,7	36	Turkey	623

Fig. 7.1 Prosperity, productivity, and effort, 2019 (*Source* OECD. *Note* GDP in current prices, Purchasing Power Parity)

Schlüter have increased income inequality as shown in Chapter 4—Fig. 7.4, Denmark still has the third least people in the low income group among OECD countries and is also performing well with a 7th place on lowest income inequality among the OECD countries. There is also only 4.7% of kids who are found in the lowest income bracket—second lowest among OECD. If we look at life earnings the income inequality is even lower. Wealth inequity has likely stagnated or declined

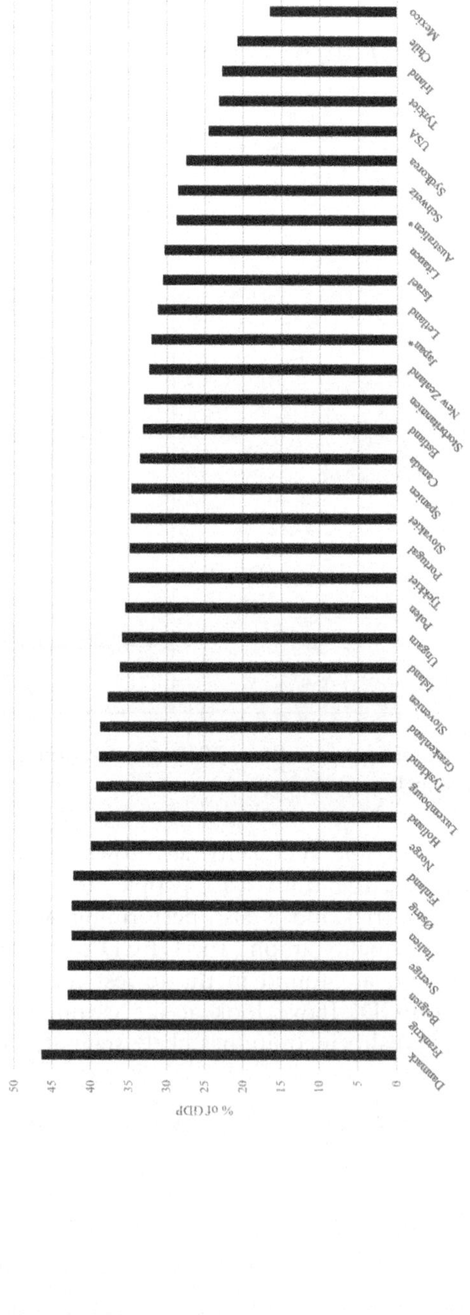

Fig. 7.2 Denmark hold the OECD championship in taxes

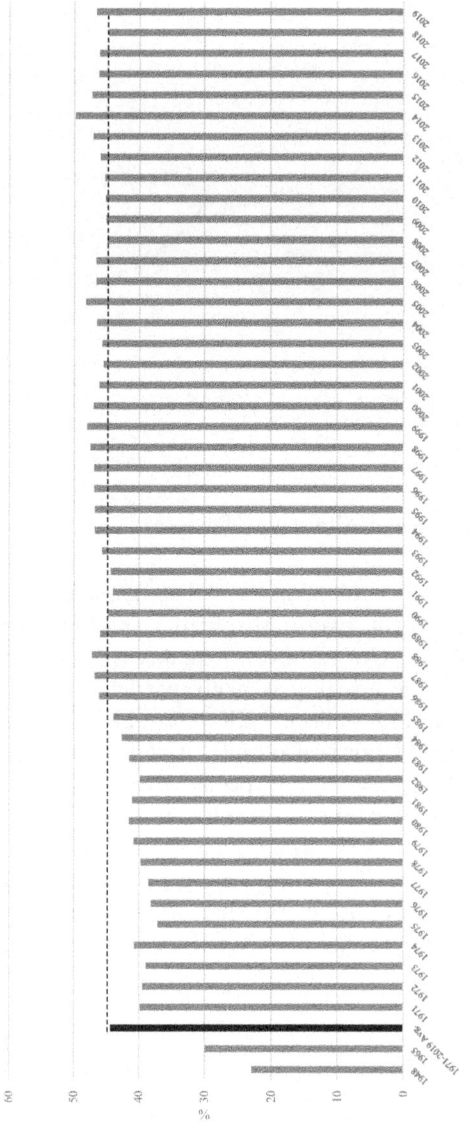

Fig. 7.3 Total tax pressure (*Source* Statistics Denmark. Numbers prior to 1971 from Danmarks Statistik [2008]: 60 år i tal - Danmark siden 2. Verdenskrig)

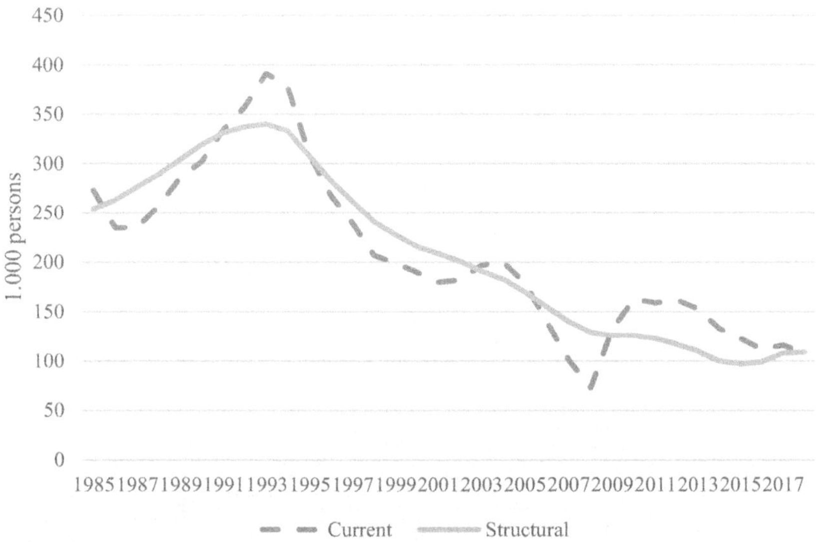

Fig. 7.4 Unemployment (*Source* Ministry of Finance)

since the nineties—mainly due to pensions.[5] Top 1% share is also significantly lower at the end of the twentieth century than the beginning as seen in Chapter 4—Fig. 7.5. Consumption equality is also high, the same is political equality. Old age equality is likely particularly high—Private pension schemes received 127 billion DKK or roughly 5.5% of GDP in 2019. Access to meaningful labor is also high—the development of unemployment is shown in Fig. 7.4—to the point where qualified labor can be hard to come by for employers. Unemployment and debt were staggering in the beginning of 1980 and the current levels are impressive policy results. Lastly, despite what some young people might feel, it is a fact that they are significantly better off than their parents in their early adulthood; a 30 year old in average earn 40% more than their parents did at that age.[6]

[5] Det Økonomiske Råd, *Dansk Økonomi, efterår 2016* (2016).

[6] Mads Lundby-Hansen, & Carl-Christian Heiberg, "Generationstyveri? De yngre generationer har højere indkomst end ældre generationer", *CEPOS* (2021). https://CEPOS.dk/artikler/generationstyveri-de-yngre-generationer-har-hoejere-indkomst-end-aeldre-generationer/, Accessed Jan 29, 2022.

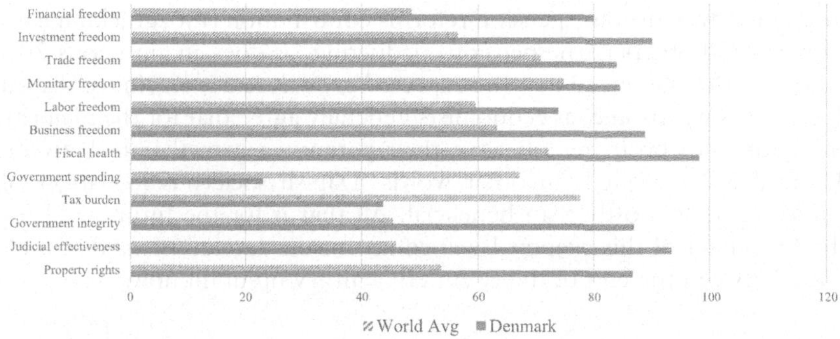

Fig. 7.5 Index of Economic Freedom 2021: Denmark vs the World average (*Source* Heritage Foundation)

While this all looks satisfactory to most, it is worth remembering the Boje thesis. Rather than comparing Denmark blindly to other OECD nations, it might be better to ask if it could have been better given Danish conditions? Some evidence suggests so. Firstly, the results mentioned above are largely the result of recent reforms—which will be elaborated on below. They are most definitely not the result of a welfare state. Secondly, the high tax rate seems to impact work effort negatively. This is particularly so, as it dampens the correlation between educational and vocational choice and life income, a tendency further fueled by a generous stipend system (the SU). In fact, noble laurate James Heckman has shown that Denmark is not better than the United States in creating social mobility with educational investments.[7] In other words, there is potential to unlock, and it might be needed, because when looking at the trend for GDP growth we have reason to worry. As seen in Chapter 4—Fig. 7.1, the twentieth century showed an average of 3% annual GDP growth in fixed prices for Denmark, but the trend is dying off. From 1986 to 2018, the underlying growth rate was only 1.1%. The reform agenda added another 0.6%, with tax reforms contributing 0.3 and labor market reforms. 0.2%. resulting in a total of 1.6. An estimate of the period 2021–2030 shows a slightly improved underlying growth rate of 1.2, but the reform picture is

[7] Rasmus Landersø, & James J. Heckman, "The Scandinavian Fantasy: The Sources of Intergenerational Mobility in Denmark and the U.S", *The Scandinavian Journal of Economics*, 119:1 (2016), pp. 178–230.

more muddy with some pension reforms contribution (tilbagtrækningsreformen) and others (Arne-pension) deducting, as does an ambitious 70% CO_2 emission target, so that the expected growth rate is an almost dismal 1.4. This is worrisome, as economists generally agree that for the majority of children to be better off than their parents, a growth rate between 1 and 1.5% is needed. In other words, Danish society is in danger of becoming more costly than beneficial. All that is for the future, and for the remainder of this chapter I will comment on developments that took place between the end of the twentieth century up untill now.

Three Key Macro Shifts

The results outlined above —good and bad—are largely driven by three key macro shifts. In this section, I will review each of them and explain why they represent a bridge between 2000 and 2020.

The Return and Stagnation of Economic Freedom

Denmark has many rules and regulations, and like many other Western states the total amount of regulations is growing which likely has negative consequences for economic growth.[8] That said, regulation regarding business formation are few, the courts are trustworthy and red tape is relatively low or automated. This is clear when we view the subindexes of Economic Freedom index in Fig. 7.5.

The process to this point was particular spearheaded by the liberal-conservative Fogh government from 2001 and is seen in Fig. 7.6, moving Denmark from the moderately free to the mostly free group at the end of millennium. However, as is seen from 2009 the development stagnated, and some industries, particularly banking, has since been met with a mindboggling amount of new rules to the point where the nature of the Danish financial business is changing; for instance, about 10% of all people employed in insurance and finance was now working mainly with compliance.[9] Yet, Denmark is not the only nation to see a stagnation in liberation after the financial crisis. In comparison Denmark is, at the time

[8] Herby, "Regelstaten".

[9] Carsten Brink, "Antallet af hvidvask og complianceanstte i bankerne eksploderer", *Finans Danmark* (Nov 17, 2019), https://finansdanmark.dk/nyheder/2019/antallet-af-hvidvask-og-complianceansatte-i-bankerne-eksploderer/, Accessed Jan 29, 2022.

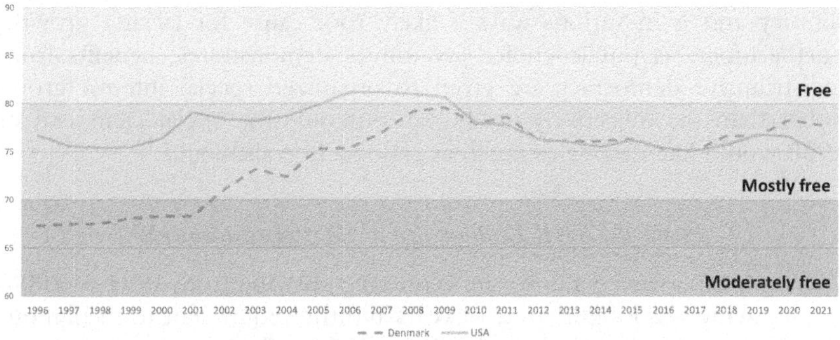

Fig. 7.6 Economic Freedom (*Source* Heritage Foundation)

of writing, more free than the United States—the traditional free-market bogyman of the Danish left. The first key macro shift is hence a return to a more favorable legislative environment for business in some ways more reminiscent of the early than late twentieth century.

The Welfare Coalition

A welfare coalition refers to the potential coalition of the subset of workers who rely primarily on tax revenue for their income via either public employment or welfare benefits. In 1970, roughly 360,000 were employed by the public sector. In 2021, this number is 830,000.[10] At the same time, the persons on welfare schemes have grown from 800,000 in 1970 to 2.2 mil in 2021. This means that the populace who are mainly dependent on redistribution via taxes has grown from 1.2 mil to over 3 mil. If we control for voting age, the result is likewise remarkable; in 1970 33% were part of the welfare coalition, in 2021 it is 64.8%. Against this background, it is impressive that the reform agenda of recent times has been possible at all. The change of voting majority from private employment to the welfare coalition occurred in the beginning of the 1980's. Today, 59% of Danes are net receivers of tax funds, and only the top income brackets are net contributors as shown in Fig. 7.7. It is a key macro shift because the development has continued in the twenty-first

[10] This is not due to COVID-19, although a small part of it can be explained by this. The number in 2020 was also growing.

century and is in various ways a likely root cause for lacking growth. Furthermore, as public choice economics demonstrates; benefits from redistributive democracy are given to organized special interest group rather than the objectively needy—an outcome the Social Democrat of 1920 would like despise as much as classical liberals would.[11]

From an SME Economy to a "Mittelstandmark"

Denmark experienced a powerful economic upswing from 1994 to 2008. The upswing was long, lasting 14 years and thus equivalent to the famous long post-war upswing from 1957 to 1972. The upswing was based on the three classical demand factors public demand, private domestic demand and private export demand and 230,000 new jobs were created.

Following the financial crisis in 2008, Denmark lost approximately 140.000 private jobs. Danish companies invested significantly less than before 2008 and less then companies in the main Danish export markets. Comparatively speaking, Danish companies invested less for a substantial period of time following 2008 as shown in Fig. 7.8. This can be worrisome for those who consider innovation as the key to future growth, as innovation often requires investments. On the other hand, it might show that Danish companies where agile and adjusted supply to expected demand.[12]

In the Danish case, it proved difficult to reestablish these jobs on basis of private domestic demand, as the Danish households from 2004 to 2008 increased the debt to one of the highest levels in Europe—131 percent of GDP. It also proved difficult to reestablish the many lost jobs on basis of the public economy as Danish Capitalism is already marked by a large public sector.

Since 2008 a political consensus has been established which recognize that a possible new upswing will be driven differently than the upswing from 1994 to 2008. It has been broadly accepted by economists, politicians, and others that the dynamics of Danish Capitalism in contrast to the mid-1990s have to be based on the private export driven demand

[11] Michael Munger, "Public Choice Economics", In: James D. Wright (ed.), *International Encyclopedia of the Social & Behavioral Sciences*, Vol. 19 (Oxford: Elsevier, 2015), pp. 534–539.

[12] If year by values is used for level comparison, the continued decline is also observed, but the true outlier is the UK, with a substantial lower baseline.

Income deciles	Gross income	Public tranfers	Public spending	Taxes and tariffs	Net contribution
1. decil	101400	82900	128100	61900	-149100
2. decil	197100	135600	145700	112600	-168700
3. decil	223200	145000	127500	129200	-143300
4. decil	261300	126600	131100	149300	-108300
5. decil	306100	98800	136400	175000	-60100
6. decil	350200	79900	136400	200500	-15800
7. decil	396100	62400	132800	228000	32800
8. decil	446600	52000	123800	259100	83300
9. decil	519100	42300	112000	303600	149300
10. decil	870700	33900	103900	512000	374200
Top 1 pct.	2189900	31800	105600	1280600	1143200

Fig. 7.7 Net contribution per income decile in 2014 (2016-levels) (*Source* Statistics Denmark and CEPOS. *Note* Calculated on actual income. Sorted on equivalent disposable income)

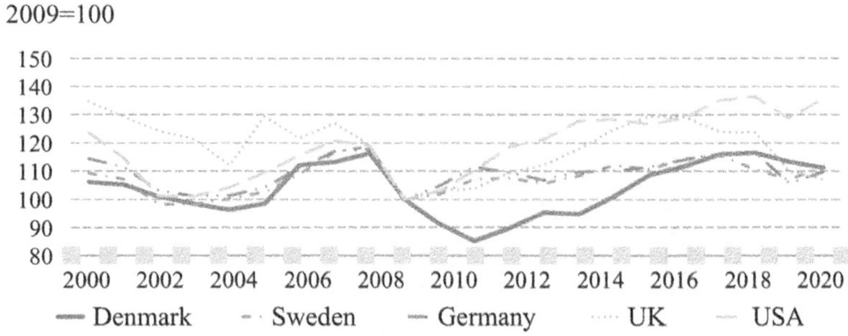

Fig. 7.8 Business investments vs GDP—indexed after the end of the 2008 Financial Crisis (*Source* Det Økonomiske Råd)

factor and consequently the private competitiveness has proven to be a key-factor, which constitutes other policies (within research, education, transport, social policies, foreign and security policies, etc.). The general label of this undertaking has been entitled "the competition state"—in Danish; konkurrencestaten.[13]

The structure of Danish business life has also changed largely driven by the global export success of key Danish companies. For most of the twentieth century, Denmark was mainly an SME economy. As shown in Fig. 7.9, this changed in the twenty-first century where the economy is now dominated by a group of the largest companies in the Top 30. In 1973, the Top 10's revenue relative to GDP was 23%, in the twenty-first century it is hovering around 40%, roughly a doubling. The names of the list are relatively stable with the companies mainly switching places among themselves. The top 10, and to a large degree the top 50 firms, also tend to share a number of characteristics. They are old—in average a 100 plus years. They are specialized and often market leading in their specialty. They are almost all global and Danish sales are insignificant. In fact, even a top 50 largest company, Novozymes, has less than 2% of its

[13] Pedersen, *Konkurrencestaten*. While there is a lot to academically critique about the "competitive state"—theory, there can be little doubt that it has had significant communicative success, including high penetration in high school social studies classes. See Chapter 1.

sales in Denmark. This means that companies with such a share could close down all Danish sales and not report it to shareholders without being in violation of good governance. While Danish political power has been increasingly centralized in Copenhagen—untill the highly debated mandated relocation of some government offices from 2016—Danish businesses remains less Copenhagen-centric. Likely this has many smaller explanations, but key among them must be the global orientation. In short, the companies that now make up the bulk of Danish economy could be described as qualitatively close to the German concept of "mittelstand". They tend to be owned or highly control by a foundation or family, long-term focus and proven survivors. They are independent, with lean hierarchies and employees who invest emotionally in their workplace. They place an emphasis on social responsibility, regional more so than national ties, and are to a large extent customer-centric.

The third key macro shift is hence that Denmark is not an SME economy, but is better viewed as comprising of a Danish version of mittlestand, less to do with size of the company, but more how it is run[14]; a Mittelstandmark.

A Shared Reform Agenda and a Paradigm Shift

In many ways, Schlüter represented the last industrial age prime minister in Denmark. During the industrialization, policy was focused on private sector conditions. As the welfare coalition grew and took over the electoral majority the focus of governments changed. In the last three decades, different governments of both the left and the right have held a shared reform agenda, but the focus of policy has been driven largely by public sector needs. The fundamental premise of the welfare state has

[14] For more on the original German construct of Mittelstand. See Ludwig Erhard, "Mittelstandspolitik", In Alexander Rüstow (ed.), *Der mittelständische Unternehmer in der Sozialen Marktwirtschaft: Wortlaut der Vorträge auf der vierten Arbeitstagung der Aktionsgemeinschaft Soziale Marktwirtschaft e.V am 17 November 1955 in Bad Godesberg* (Ludwigsburg: 1956), pp. 51–61; Jeffery Fear, "Straight outta Oberberg: Transforming Mid-Sized Family Firms into Global Champions 1970–2010", *Jahrbuch für Wirtschaftsgeschichte*, 53:1 (2012), pp. 125–169; Hartmut Berghoff, *Moderne Unternehmensgeschichte: Eine Themen- und Theorieorientierte Einführung* (Berlin: Walter de Gruyter GmbH, 2016); David B. Audretsch, Erik E. Lehmann, & Julian Schenkenhofer, "Internationalization Strategies of Hidden Champions: Lessons from Germany", *Multinational business review*, 26:1 (2018), pp. 2–24.

1973					
Danish GDP total 1.017					
	Revenue	**Employees**	**Founding Yea**	**HQ**	**Main industry**
ØK	77,8	36474	1897	Copenhagen	Shipping
APM-Maersk	54,3	13675	1904	Copenhagen	Shipping
FDB (COOP)	22,3	7760	1896	Copenhagen	Retail
Ess-Food	19,4	500	1950	Copenhagen	Agriculture
DfB (Carlsberg)	14,9	7500	1847	Copenhagen	Food & Drinks
KFK	12,6	686	1896	Aarhus	Agriculture
DLG	12	1416	1898	Fredericia	Agriculture
P&T	11,4	17369	1624	Copenhagen	Postal service
J. Lauritzen	10,9	9029	1884	Copenhagen	Shipping
FL Smith	10,3	5100	1882	Copenhagen	Heavy machinary
Total / Total / Avg / Copenhagen share	**245,9**	**99509**	**1868**	**80%**	
Top 10 / GDP: 24%					

1990					
Danish GDP total 1.282					
	Revenue	**Employees**	**Founding Yea**	**HQ**	**Main industry**
APM-Maersk	65,5	17822	1904	Copenhagen	Shipping
FDB (COOP)	33,7	14405	1896	Copenhagen	Retail / production
ØK	24,6	15888	1897	Copenhagen	Trading / shipping
P&T	21,1	33462	1624	Copenhagen	Postal service
MD (Arla)	19,9	5501	1882	Aarhus	Food & Drinks
Danisco	19,4	12744	1872	Nakskov	Ingredients
FL Smith	17,7	10937	1882	Copenhagen	Heavy machinary
J. Lauritzen	17,6	12200	1884	Copenhagen	Shipping
Carlsberg	16,3	12192	1847	Copenhagen	Food & Drinks
ISS	14,6	108200	1901	Copenhagen	Facility management
Total / Total / Avg / Copenhagen share	**250,4**	**243351**	**1859**	**80%**	
Top 10 / GDP: 20%					

2010					
Danish GDP total 1.745					
	Revenue	**Employees**	**Founding Yea**	**HQ**	**Main industry**
APM-Maersk	315,4	108110	1904	Copenhagen	Shipping
ISS	74,1	506693	1901	Copenhagen	Facility management
Novo Nordisk	60,8	29423	1923	Copenhagen	Pharma
Carlsberg	60,1	41402	1847	Copenhagen	Food & Drinks
Dong (Ørsted)	54,6	5800	1973	Fredericia	Energy
United Shipping and Trading	51,6	872	1876	Middelfart	Shipping
Vestas	51,5	22216	1945	Århus	Renewables
Arla Foods	49	16215	1882	Aarhus	Food & Drinks
Wrist Group	45,2	1256	2000	Aalborg	Shipping
Danish Crown	45,2	23305	1970	Randers	Food & Drinks
Total / Total / Avg / Copenhagen share	**807,5**	**755292**	**1922**	**40%**	
Top 10 / GDP: 46%					

2020					
Danish GDP total 2330					
	Revenue	**Employees**	**Founding Yea**	**HQ**	**Main industry**
APM-Maersk	244	80000	1904	Copenhagen	Shipping
Novo Nordisk	122	41100	1923	Copenhagen	Pharma
Vestas	92,9	17000	1945	Århus	Renewables
ISS	78,5	500000	1901	Copenhagen	Facility management
United Shipping and Trading	76,3	2500	1876	Middelfart	Shipping
Danish Crown	60,8	23000	1970	Randers	Food & Drinks / Agriculture
Salling Group	60	50000	1960	Århus	Retail
Carlsberg	58,5	40000	1847	Copenhagen	Food & Drinks
Ørsted	56,2	6500	1973	Fredericia	Energy
DLG	51,3	6600	1898	Fredericia	Agriculture
Total / Total / Avg / Copenhagen share	**900,5**	**766700**	**1920**	**40%**	
Top 10 / GDP: 39%					

Fig. 7.9 Top 10 Danish companies from share of economy—sample years (*Source* Initial analysis developed by Martin Iversen [Copenhagen Business School], updated by author. *Note* bDKK, 2010 values)

not been challenged, but rather the reform have been attempts to optimize the model. Nyrup Rasmussen lost the election when he prioritized reforms to much too fast for some voters, and Fogh learned to optimize the approach to reforms with an almost religious devotion to the median-voter theorem. This from a prime minister who in his youth is credited with a book called "From Social State to Minimal State".[15] The reforms of the 21st century have largely been successful; more people have found employment, motivated largely by cuts in welfare allowance, and public finances have improved—but at the same time the public sector also grew. The biggest issue for the reform agenda has likely been the relation to inequality. When people join the labor force, income inequality rises. This trade-off is shown in Fig. 7.10, even more so as the incentive often was welfare cuts.

Also of note was the approach toward tax reform. Inspired by the never realized "Plan of The Century" form Schülter, Nyrup shifted the tax burden from labor to consumption. Fogh later made the famous innovation of Tax stop, whereby the tax burden was not allowed to increase. This is particularly important, as it created stable and reliable institutions, and is likely a larger part of the reason for the prosperity in the 21st century than is often acknowledged. While critiqued at the time—a criticism it should be noted that was often technically well founded in a narrow theoretical sense—it worked to increase public sector efficiency and private sector trust. Particularly as it put a stop to the ever-growing municipal tax rate.

Within economics, taxation debates often revolve around the Laffer-curve. The concept that there is a limit to how high effective taxation can be. The precise cut off point is hard to measure, and ultimately depend on individual utility. It is however highly likely that the breaking point was likely reached toward the end of the twentieth century. Particularly on the corporate tax where tax revenue rose, as the rate was later decreased as shown in Fig. 7.11. Also, the level of unofficial economy appears to have fallen to half its end of century level. The reasons are manifold, including more active regulation, but the continued lowering of marginal tax rates likely played a part in this as well. The move toward lower marginal tax rate from a staggering 73% (up from 2.5% in 1903) was undertaken by

[15] Anders Fogh Rasmussen, *Fra socialstat til minimalstat: En liberal strategi* (København: Samleren, 1993).

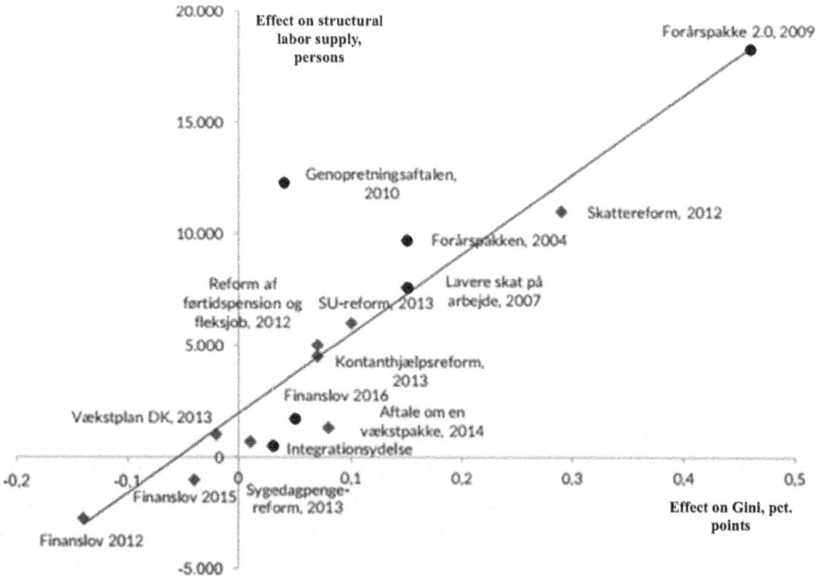

Fig. 7.10 Effect of reforms on labor supply vs income inequality (*Source* CEPOS, Fordelingspolitisk redegørelse. *Note* Square indicates leftwing governments. Circle indicates right-wing governments)

Schluter and continued by Poul Nyrup Rasmussen (prime minister 1993–2001) and Anders Fogh Rasmussen (prime minister 2001–2009) to the so far lowest point of 56 pct. in 2010. Since then, it has increased slightly until the Paradigm shift. Today, numerically speaking, more people with no or only trade education pay the top tax (a higher level tax, above a certain income level) than academics.[16]

What was harder to control was the public expenses which continued to grow. Prime Minister Lars Løkke Rasmussen had to oversee a reform to reestablish the Danish economy after the 2008 Finansiel Crisis which he did efficiently, primarily driven by labor market reform and tighter public sector budgets.

[16] Mads Lundby-Hansen, & Thomas Due Bostrup, "Flere ufaglærte og faglærte betaler topskat end akademikere", *CEPOS*, https://CEPOS.dk/artikler/flere-ufaglaerte-og-faglaerte-end-akademikere-betaler-topskat/, Accessed Jan 29, 2022.

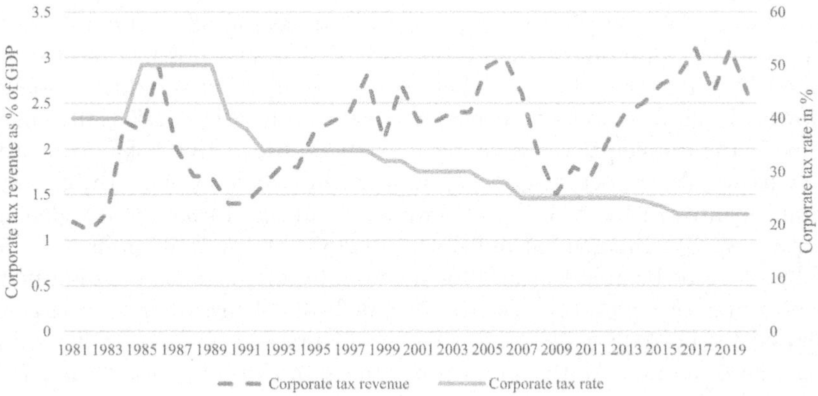

Fig. 7.11 Corporate tax rate and revenue

The paradigm of economic responsibility via continued reform to safeguard the welfare state was in many ways cemented with the first female Prime Minster Helle Thorning-Schmidt (b.1966) whose government noted in their policy aims that "[our economic policy] is a continuation of the previous liberal-conservative government's in the widest way, including their already initiated reforms".[17] The policy included a further lowering of corporate taxes. On the institutional level, a complete reform of the municipality level had also been undertaken by Løkke.

Municipality Reform II—The Difficulty of Public Efficiency

The Danish hospital system became increasingly distressed during the 1990s, and after the turn of the millennium, things went completely sour with extensive waiting list problems and poor quality achievements in international comparisons. This substantial problem for the welfare state was to set in motion an almost all-encompassing public reorganization. With the municipal reform in 1970, it was mainly the 14 county municipalities (Danish: Amter) as well as Copenhagen and Frederiksberg that took care of the hospital operations. After 2000, Studies showed that this structure entailed unrealized specialization and economies of scale.

[17] Regeringen, "Et Danmark, der står sammen", *Regeringsgrundlag oktober 2011* (2011).

In addition, it was realized that preventive efforts should be intensified. A government-appointed commission presented several possible models in 2004.[18] A crucial point was whether the county level should be closed down all together, so that the hospitals were made a state task at the same time as the municipalities were given extended preventive tasks. Not least due to Social Democratic opposition, it was not possible to get the county municipalities disbanded, but they were instead transformed into 5 almost pure hospital management units, The Regions. As these Regions did not fully prove to be able to stand for the establishment of the ongoing new generation of superhospitals, the overall hospital task in reality largely shifted to the state while preserving the Regions as political bodies with no power to tax. At the same time, the municipalities, for their part, proved nearly incapable of delivering satisfying results within the area of prevention. Likewise, it turned out that regions and municipalities were not effectively able to cooperate.

Especially in the first years after 2007, there was in fact a significant productivity development in the hospital system. A significant factor here was the introduction of so-called free choice of hospital in 2003. Patients were given the right to freely choose a place of treatment, including at a private hospital, if the "home hospital" could not offer treatment within 30 days. This provided a tremendous incentive for public hospitals. Since then, in the absence of follow-up incentives, public hospitals have managed to manage waiting lists, so that the growth of private hospitals has stagnated. The inability of the Folketing to have the Regions closed down, and the weakened pressure on further productivity growth in the hospital area, made it possible in 2019 for the Regions to pressure the government to abandon further general demands for increased productivity.

With the structural reform in 2007, the number of municipalities was instantly reduced from 273 to 98. The upscaling of the administrative units was not least justified by the fact that the labor market task was to be left entirely to the municipalities. Here, a state system had previously functioned, which to a large extent was effectively controlled by the social partners, and after high youth unemployment rates after 1973, an ever-larger municipal system had been expanded. However, the municipal effort after 2007 quickly proved to be of highly fluctuating quality,

[18] Strukturkommissionen, "Betænkning nr. 1434", *Strukturkommissionens betænkning* (2004).

and the new system became to a not insignificant extent a system for handling people more or less permanently outside the labor market. No less so, as the current level of unemployment is impressively low (at the time of writing) and the potential sanctioning of unemployment benefits depend on the individual social worker attached to the case. One analysis published by the Danish Employer Organization calculated that only 0.1% of recipients of unemployment benefits were sanctioned, despite the fact that the number of recipients who did not live up to the requirement for receiving benefits was likely more than 11 times larger.

The larger municipalities also proved to be unable to take advantage of economies of scale to a greater extent, and the financing system was also designed so that it did not assume economies of scale. The largest municipalities would thus run a direct risk if they uncovered that in the real world there were economies of scale. They could risk the effect being put into the financing system. On the other hand, the new larger municipalities proved to be able to exploit political advantages by the fact that the individual municipalities now, for many, became heavy political players in their own right proved so that they could gain a foothold directly at Christiansborg (the parliament). It became more logical for municipalities to complain about their special conditions in the corridors of parliaments than to do something about the atrocities at home. The municipalities hence moved further in the direction of being lobby organizations. Incomplete institutions, the self-interest of the political system and general short-sightedness all in all made the streamlining of the welfare state a very difficult matter. The only thing that did work was a system of fines for municipalities that went over budget—this stopped the constant overspending and even improved the result compared to the budget on the national level.

In short, the reform paradigm was a success. Figure 7.12 shows the reforms form 2001 and their effect on labor supply. The welfare state went from effectively bankruptcy in 1980 to excess solvency by 2019—when Lars Løkke Rasmussen handed over the keys to the Prime Minister car to Mette Frederiksen the national budgets was overfunded by 23 bDKK. This is likely the richest and most economically well consolidated the Danish state have been in recorded history. Yet a paradigm shift was coming.

	Full time employee
Flere i arbejde, 2002	10,000
Forårspakken, 2004	9,700
2001-2005 total	**19,700**
En ny chance til alle, 2005	4,500
Velfærdsaftalen, 2006 (Virkningen er på 247.000 fuldtidspersoner i 2040)	105,000
Lavere skat på arbejde, 2007	7,600
2005-2007 total	**117,100**
Jobplanen, 2008	3,600
Aftale om nedbringelse af sygefraværet, 2008	4,000
Forårspakke 2.0, 2009	18,300
Genopretningsaftalen, 2010	12,300
Aftalen om senere tilbagetrækning, 2011	60,000
2007-2011 total	**98,200**
Finanslovsaftale 2012	-4,500
Energiaftale, 2012	-500
Skattereformen, 2012	15,800
Reform af førtidspension og fleksjob, 2012	7,000
Reform af SU-systemet, 2013	6,000
Aftale om reform af kontanthjælpssystemet, 2013	6,000
Aftale om Vækstplan DK (øvrige elementer bortset fra SU og kontanthjælp), 2013	1,300
Forlig om en reform af sygedagpengesystemet, 2013	1,300
Forlig om reform af beskæftigelsesindsatsen, 2013	800
Refusionsomlægning (Reform af beskæftigelsesindsatsen), 2014	3,000
Aftale om en vækstpakke, 2014	1,300
Finanslovsaftale 2015	-1,000
2011-2015 total	**36,500**
Jobreform fase I (kontanthjælpsloft), 2015	700
Integrationsydelse, 2015	500
Aftale om et tryggere dagpengesystem, 2015	-850
FL16 (lavere registreringsafgift), 2015	500
FL17 (lavere registreringsafgift), 2016	350
PSO-aftalen, 2016	750
Aftale om flere år på arbejdsmarkedet, 2017	700
Aftale om omlægning af bilafgifter, 2017	600
Aftale om ny ferielov, 2017	-1,400
Erhvervs- og iværksætterinitiativer, 2017	350
FL18 (sorgorlov), 2017	-100
Skatteaftale, 2018	1,200
Mediepolitisk aftale, 2018	-100
Energiaftale, 2018	200
Regelforenkling af beskæftigelsesindsatsen, 2018	-200
FL19, 2018	1,350
Aftale om seniorpension, 2019	-500
2015-2019 total	**4,050**
FL20, 2019	-900
Arne-Pension, 2020	-9,800
Aftale om grøn omstilling af vejtransporten, 2020	550
Other initiatives, 2020	-300
2019-2020 All together	**-10,450**
TOTAL	**265,100**

Fig. 7.12 List of recent reforms in electoral periods, labor supply effect, 2025 effect

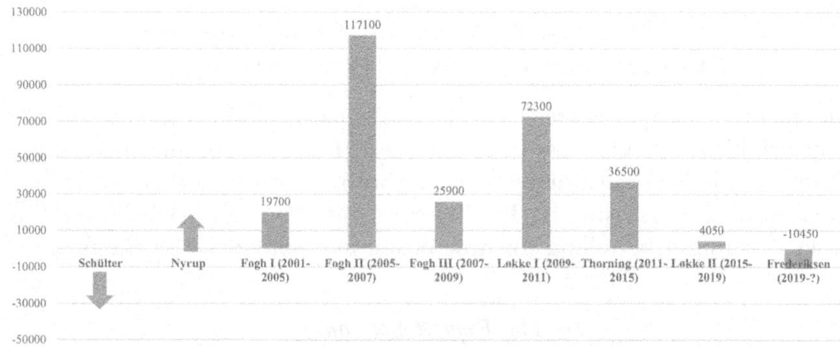

Fig. 7.13 Labor supply results under modern Prime Ministers (*Source* Finansministeriet. Cepos. *Note* Both Schulter and Nyrup ***aimed*** to increase labor supply, but we do not know the precise effect. It was likely slightly negative for Schulter (there was other more pressing issues), and significantly positive for Nyrup due to benefit cuts and decreasing the marginal tax rate)

The Possible Paradigm Shift?

With the election of Mette Frederiksen, a new economic paradigm shift potentially took place in Danish economy. As the first Prime Minister, she went to the ballot box with a plan to reduce the labor market participation, a policy that has indeed been implemented. It cannot be stressed how significant this is. In Fig. 7.13, the effect on labor market participations under each Prime Minister since Schlüter is noted. Precise measures for Schlüter and Nyrup do not exist, but while Schlüter did not manage an increase in participation, it was a desired policy aim to do so. Since Nyrup all Prime Ministers, even Løkke II who faced a de facto dysfunctional parliamentary support and already really low employment, have raised labor market participation. Further to this change, the platform of Mette Frederiksen called for an end to traditional reforms of carrot and stick.[19] She has also raised taxes 39 times in two years—despite having an already overfunded budget.

[19] She has established a committee to suggest so-called 2nd generation reforms, but what they are, how they will work and on what is at the time of writing not established. An Ydelseskommision was also established to look at the welfare benefit system.

The Value War; Immigration Skeptics and Activist Foreign Policy

Denmark's place in the world also changed in the twenty-first century, likely in two very different ways. Business became increasingly global, while internal politics became both increasing nationalistic, and internationally activistic. As I will argue, this produced some interesting cases that might be telling for how businesses will behave in the future.

The Export Economy

In 1970, export of goods and services amounted to 28% of GDP, up to 50% in 2010. An impressive development particularly when considering the expansive public sector in the same period. This is a testimony to an increasing exposure to a global value chain. In short, while export has always been a significant element of Danish prosperity, the twenty-first century saw a major increase. It is therefore important to ask, how important national belonging is to Danish companies going forward. The money is not being made in Denmark.

The Value War, Immigration and Activist Foreign Policy

While the fundamental nature of Danish companies and business life has changed toward globalism, the national policy seems to have gone the other way. The election of Fogh, in the system change of 2001 began the so-called "value war".[20] A populist fueled center-right project centered around what it meant to be Danish and in policy terms focused highly on immigration. Immigration laws were toughened to the often despair of business interests (but open borders and universal welfare rights is a poor match from a budget point of view). Denmark began following an expansive foreign military policy alongside the United States. The populist immigration skeptic Danish People Party (Dansk Folkeparti) became one of the largest political influences with a key focus on immigration prevention and welfare state preservation.

One example of the impact of the value war for business was the infamous 2005 Cartoon Crisis. In 2005, a debate was brewing in the cultural

[20] Schjørring & Jannerup, *Værdikæmperne: slaget om danskernes sjæl: VK-regeringerne 2001–2011.*

circles as to whether artists would draw the prophet Muhammed. Most artists preferred not to or flat out refused. While some cited tolerance concerns, many also explicit said, that they feared the consequence from radical Muslims, as it is prohibited to depict the prophet in the eyes of many muslims. The Danish newspaper *Jyllands-Posten* decided to publish 12 satirical drawings of Muhammed as part of the debate. This set fire to the Middle East. In a letter to Prime Minister Fogh, 11 ambassadors from Muslim countries demanded that he took action against *Jyllands—Posten* and others, including a minister and a member of parliament. The Prime Minister refused, as such actions would be in volition of the Danish constitution. On December 29th, the Arabic League expressed criticisms of Denmark for the handling of the case. December was further full of strikes and demonstration in the Middle East world, and a boycott toward Danish goods followed in January 2006. The boycott had significant consequences and even pushed the Danish Federation of Industry to pressure *Jyllands-Posten* to issue an apology. On the other side, a smaller conservative campaign in support if Denmark called "Buy Danish" erupted in the United States.

The Cartoon Crisis in many ways changed what it meant to be a Danish firm in a global world. In the past, it had mainly been an advantage for trading with Western countries; a non-threatening country with stable institutions, trustworthy merchants and good courts. Now companies had to answer for actions they neither had little control of nor interest in. Danish companies have been quick to adapt the fashionable tenant of CSR, diversity and "going green", but they have also had to face tough decisions as a consequence. Examples are many; signing contracts prohibiting trade with Jews in order to secure trade with Muslim countries—and then doing it anyway. The relation to civil rights abuses in China, an often-debated topic in Danish media, supporting gay rights in Denmark, but not in the former eastern bloc. The dilemmas are many, and Immanuel Kant would rightly be horrified by the behavior of many modern business leaders.

While the response to globalization for Danish firms has been to embrace it, the response has largely been opposite for the populace, the state somewhere in the middle. A further joker is the increasingly strategical important Greenland—which US President Donald Trump (b. 1946) even offered to buy like the Virgin Island some 100 years earlier. As Danish society is paid for by increasingly global companies, the future relation to policy desires in Denmark is likely to be contested.

Housing, Real Estate and Crime

While this grouping might seem odd, it makes sense and will need to be commented on in sequence. During the twentieth century, the real estate market developed—as expected—rapidly. The Social Democratic party wanted to improve on the often dismal living conditions of the working class and prioritize urban sanitations and council estate development. Toward the Poul Nyrup Rasmussen further liberalized the housing market, fueling the transformation of particular Copenhagen from urban wasteland to a globally desirable city. Unfortunately for the original public housing vision, the economic growth enabled the more skilled and affluent parts of the working class and lower-middle class to move to the many new single-family homes (parcelhuse) constructed from around the 1960 onwards, foregoing the council estates. This was in large part made possible by the Danish realkredit system for lending. The system dates back to 1757, but took off around the 1850s. It has a couple of design elements worth noting. While the loan is granted in a real estate asset, the obligation is personal. That means that should the value of the house for example fall below the purchase price and the loan taker default on payments, the borrower can be stuck with the remaining debt even after the house is sold. This system is less flexible than e.g. the American where loans are tied directly to asset use rights. On the other hand, the housing loans are European style options. This means they can be called at any moment by the burrower but not vice versa. This means that the burrower can refinance whenever terms, like interest, is more advantageous. This also drives up prices in high growth areas such as Copenhagen where an apartment purchase in 1975 can yield a return of non-inflation adjusted 2000%. In short, the real estate market in Denmark in the twenty-first century is highly divided between some areas around the larger towns having experience growth, while in more rural areas the return can be negative.

But what happened to the council estates? The remaining inhabitants consisting largely of what Marxist theory would call the lumpe proletariat. However, as immigrant workers were invited to fill the ranks of the growing industry started to arrive and the later refugees too, many were placed in the council estate. This led to racial disturbances doing the

1980's in particular. From these disturbance, and a need to protect non-Danish residents grew the first street gangs, like Warriors,[21] a movement not unlike what is seen with the emergence of US prison gangs.[22]

The mere existence of organized crime in Denmark is to some puzzling, as organized crime tends to associated with weak regulatory power, low trust, and few outside options. Towards the end of the twentieth century, the crime scene was largely controlled by biker gangs, and two great biker conflicts emerged in 1983–1985 and 1994–1997. However, with the crack down on the semi-legal marijuana market in the free town Christiania (in central Copenhagen) the market for organized crime erupted, and immigrant street gangs emerged as strong independent contenders, to the point where particularly the 2010s have seen intense violent, and ongoing, gang warfare. This despite a welfare state providing free education and other generous possibilities available to all.

The Rebirth of Entrepreneurship?

A major change in regards to both business and policy in the twenty-first century was a renewed interest in promoting entrepreneurship. At the end of the twentieth century, the once proud commercial nation had arrived at a point where entrepreneurs were distrusted and slightly scorned. This has changed—particularly due to intense governmental focus during the Fogh governments. Today, firm creation rates are high and many places of education offer mandatory entrepreneurship education.

Denmark has created 5 unicorns in the past two decades: Zendesk, Unity, Just Eat, Sitecore, Tradeshift—companies each estimated to be worth more than 1 billion USD. They are all digital companies, and all left Denmark to grow. These 5 unicorns alone are estimated by some analysis to equal the market cap of AP Møller—Maersk. The top 50 Danish tech companies have created 50,000 jobs and value for 500 billion DKK in the last 3 years. This sounds promising for the future, but half of the above 50 companies have also moved—including seven in the top 10. The value has gone abroad. The reason is hard to disentangle. The large pension funds are almost non-exposed to start-up and venture funding. Tax rules punish

[21] Sløk-Madsen et al., "The Organization of Danish Gangs: A Transaction Cost Approach".

[22] David Skarbek, *The Social Order of the Underworld: How Prison Gangs Govern the American Penal System* (Oxford: Oxford University Press, 2014).

risk taking, while not softening losses. The state has attempted to make up for this lack of private funding, but state investors are poor substitutes, and often financing schemes become political victims, so as to be more focused on greenwashing or diversity than profit and consumer demand. Finally, the Danish mini-exchange First North has been haunted by scandals, not least since the really successful companies seem more than able to raise funds internationally leaving only the bottom of barrel for First North—some would claim.

Young people are often more mobile than older people. If the same is true for firms—and it likely is—it is worrisome that companies that can move, do move. As argued earlier in this chapter the global nature of Danish businesses has intensified in the twenty-first century.

Lobbyism and the Twenty-First Century State

Likely unbeknownst to most Danes, the Danish constitution offers very few universal individual rights. One of the few is freedom of trade, including the requirement to offer compensation if such a right is violated by nationalization or similar policy initiatives. It is therefore worrying that parliament so easily could alter compensation frameworks just prior to the COVID-19 lockdowns. Proving sadly, that all laws require moral habitus by their administrators to be upheld. It is also worrying that the schemes designed to help businesses during lockdowns were very poorly designed and implemented—created by bureaucrats with little understanding of a P/L statement, customer relations or competition. In 2021, the Danish public sector employs the most lobbyists and journalist, and the public sector and its employees did not suffer many consequences compared to private sector and particularly self-employed people, from lockdowns.

In this book, I have at times described the intimate relationship between state power and Danish business interest. As the world has become truly global for some firms however, what we might see now is perhaps a split where on the one hand we have the global companies who almost view being Danish as an accident of history more so than a raison d'être. On the other hand is the companies that are largely exposed to Danish conditions. Media companies are locked in a goliath struggle between the intense government funding of the media—there are more journalist in public sector employment, than in private and the Danish National Broadcasting Corporation is way ahead of the curve in terms of wages and benefits—and the success of international tech giants like Google and Facebook. They often call for and lobby for national intervention. Another example is Falck—an emergency service provider founded in 1906 and for a long time almost synonymous with ambulances in Denmark. When they lost a tender in the Southern region of Denmark to Dutch company Bios they responded not commercially, but politically. They launched an intensive PR campaign, joined forces with union representatives and took the sick citizens de facto hostage in a nasty and devious political campaign that crossed the line into criminal behavior—resulting in a record high 30 million DKK fine. From a management theory point of view, it seems likely that Falck had fallen into a complacency trap and over time altered their core competences from commercial to political.[23] The main business organization, DA and DI, has also increasingly moved away from suggesting free market or structural reform, to instead seeking economic relief and direct support for those businesses and industries. Particularly for those firms still mainly exposed to the Danish market.

Conclusion

In many ways, historically speaking, 2001 was a true cut-off point between the centuries. While business increasingly turned global, political interest increasingly turned national. Politics became less focused on private sector arrangements, and more on securing the welfare state model. In this book, I have repeatedly argued that whatever institutional arrangement that is politically favored in Denmark, it is economically dependent on free competitive businesses. Both the modernization of the first half of the twentieth century and the later expense required for a universal welfare state was carried largely by business. These businesses—to different degrees—saw favorably on being Danish or profited from it. It is not quite clear if this will remain the case in the future as successful companies today are more global than national, and politicians who cater for a national audience must tread extra carefully in the future in the constant Danish trade-off between state and market— only time will tell if policymakers manage this well.

[23] Chapter 4 in Stefan Kirkegaard Sløk-Madsen, *Entrepreneurial Judgment and Commercialization* (Frederiksberg: Copenhagen Business School, 2019).

Not since absolutism has the state been so internally focused. Back then such a policy focus initiated a downward spiral. It is also worrisome, because as Acemoglu and Robinson point out, the goal of twenty-first century mainstream policy is to walk the narrow corridor between effective state power and a market-based civil society.[24] Denmark is a prime case study for this theory—Danes should hope that Denmark is a positive case for the theory in the twenty-first century too.

[24] Daron Acemoglu, James A. Robinson, *The Narrow Corridor: How Nations Struggle for Liberty* (London: Penguin, 2019).

Concluding Remarks

This book is written as individual chapters in the hope that they can easily and quickly serve scholars and policymakers with various interests in and motivations for understanding Danish capitalism, mixed economy institutional antecedents, or innovism. That said the book did outline three research questions and I will attempt to answer them here based on the book's review of policy and history. Before doing so, I will raise a further point of debate: Was Danish capitalism a success in the twentieth century and for whom?

The Damned Victory

Maybe the mixed economy status of Denmark post 2000 is the ultimate trade-off between individual and mob, between market and state, between chaos and order? Or at least, it might be the ultimate Danish trade-off. Maybe Nelson (see Chapter 4) was on to something, but in a slightly different way. The welfare state is historically founded, but not in religion, but from the core of Danish social insight as written in stone by King Harold Bluetooth (see Chapter 2). That having been said, is such a nationalist insight worth much in a global business world?

When life-long union activist Thomas Nielsen (1917–1992) resigned as chairman of LO in February of 1982 his speech instantly became memorable and mythological. Almost to the level of H.P. Holst's famous

© The Editor(s) (if applicable) and The Author(s), under exclusive license to Springer Nature Switzerland AG 2022

S. K. Sløk-Madsen, *Danish Capitalism in the 20th Century*, Palgrave Studies in Economic History,
https://doi.org/10.1007/978-3-031-04267-6

word's about external loses and internal gains (see Chapter 4). Beside praising the non-revolutionary approach to labor market improvements so successfully undertaken by the majority of Danish unions and the left, the most famous part of the speech bears quoting:

> *If I look back to the time in the 30'ties when I started as a shaper apprentice and compare that time to now, then my claim will be that I along with thousand of others, belong to a generation have been damn well victorious. And that is a life well worth remembering.*[1]

There is ominous double meaning in the "damned well victorious"-phrasing (Danish: "sejret ad helvede til godt"). It is debatable whether Nielsen himself meant this as a paronomasia. Nevertheless, the unions and the Social Democratic party had managed to change the fundamental institutional logic from liberal to social. Such fundamental changes are rare in history. But the dream was hardly materialized before its very life was threatened by economic realities. However, since the dominant institutional logic had now been changed, even the rightwing parties of parliament embraced the welfare state and it seems that the twentieth century was indeed but a further chapter in the story started with the Jellinge Stone in 965; the market horse had to carry the dangerous but ideally protective state snake.

Did Denmark Max Out?

Another interesting way of concluding this book is to ask if Denmark maxed out? Could the nation have been richer for instance? The Boje thesis argues for it, and it is interesting to note the speed and efficiency with which the dominant institutional logic changed. If the reader will allow, I will make a compassion. Until Alfred the Great, England was not a unified kingdom, and in fact the role and indeed relevance of the joint royal institution remained challenged even after Alfred, but slowly the institution of a common English king became unquestioned. But for a long time, the trade-offs involved with centralized shared monarchy were debatable: as the court physician to Henry I of England (1068–1135),

[1] Authors translation."Thomas Nielsens (LO) afslutningsreplik 16. februar 1982.", *Danmarkshistorien.dk,* (2011), https://danmarkshistorien.dk/leksikon-og-kilder/vis/materiale/thomas-nielsens-lo-afslutningsreplik-16-februar-1982/, Accessed Jan. 29, 2022.

Petrus Alfonsi (1062–1140) expressed "*A king is like a fire, If you are too close, you burn; if you are too far away, you freeze*".[2] Maybe the attitude towards the universal welfare state is similar today: If you are too close, you will burn, if you are too far way you will freeze. The quote interesting also works for free markets in Danish capitalism. This is why the paradigm shift is potentially—if carried out—revolutionary. Has the Social Democratic party temporarily reversed to a pre-Anker Jørgensen economic illiteracy or is it the shape of a new change in dominant institutional logic? A step out of the narrow corridor between state and civil society that has helped generated Danish prosperity when followed.[3]

It is worrisome because the current Social Democratic government during the COVID-19 pandemic has shown an uncanny willingness to use state power very rarely seen in the twentieth century. Particularly against commercial interests: potentially violating the constitution by ordering the forced slaughter of all commercial mink and banning the mink business. This without legal authority and with dire disregard for the core and most holy Danish civil right, freedom of trade. Furthermore, the whole framing on the narrative regarding lock-downs too is also odd for a historian of Danish capitalism; the debate was framed, as when the state would allow society to reopen. Danes well into the twentieth century would likely have prefer to phase the debate, as how long society could allow the state keep society closed? If indeed what we are seeing is the state expressing superiority over business and markets, it is an even more dangerous path for policy today than at previous times. Unlike earlier in history, capital and business is highly mobile and global now—as illustrated with the growth start-ups leaving Denmark, low national sales for the largest companies, and an increasingly global workforce. The Danish state is less and less relevant for modern companies, yet the Danish state is more and more dependent on the economy as state expenses rise from the Baumol decease and voters demand for service also rises.

While aspirations of the universal welfare state were noble—the majority should protect economically exposed individuals, the sad truth is that now the Danish welfare state is the exploitation of a minority of net tax payers by the majority of net tax users. This welfare coalition majority

[2] Carolly Erickson, "Royal Panoply: Brief Lives of the English Monarchs", *Reference & Research Book News* (Portland: Ringgold, Inc, 2006).

[3] Daron Acemoglu, James A. Robinson, *The Narrow Corridor: How Nations Struggle for Liberty* (London: Penguin, 2019).

is not uniform however, there are fundamental different interests among welfare recipients and public sector employees. Therefore, it is an interesting question for the next decade how this underlying power struggle will play out, and to what degree firms will still front the bill. So Denmark likely maxed out in redistribution, but not in prosperity.

Why Did Danish Capitalism Foster so Different Companies that Proved Globally Competitive?

The question is likely that the market was allowed to specialize. A stable home market with well-grounded institutions created fertile growth conditions for ideas—often imported—and allowed such ideas to generate rents. Increasingly as the state started the welfare state experiment, the companies enjoyed some initial benefits, such as an increased talent pool from institutionalized daycare. But as the world became increasingly global from the 1990s, the companies' focus became increasingly global too—to the point where the link to Denmark is for most less day by day, and while Denmark can still create interesting new companies to an impressive degree, these companies (are smart enough to) leave early.

How Were These Companies Impacted by—and Did They Impact—Danish Capitalism?

Scandinavian capitalism has been called a competitive periphery.[4] This was likely the case for Denmark in the nineteenth to twentieth century. From a poor and challenged outset, the country transformed to meet the new conditions as a small nation in a minor corner of the World. The first half of the twentieth century and the patriotic capitalists even helped save Denmark as an independent nation. This is likely explained by the personal preferences of the specific business people, but also the commercial advantages large companies at the time gained from a close relation to Danish policy. The second part of the twentieth century is more complex. While the politicians and the state managed to realign from a German orientation to an Anglo-Saxon one, the state organization also joined forces with agriculture and workers special interests in the formation of the welfare state. While providing initial benefits, Danish business

[4] Fellman et al., *Creating Nordic Capitalism: The Business History of a Competitive Periphery*.

also had to struggle to contain the power of special interest groups over the productive economy. They defended their right to shareholder property and management but had to accept large scale redistribution in return. This became an integral part of Danish capitalism: A free market that pays for a redistributive state. What Danish capitalism with the global orientation of markets in the twenty-first century will be, is more questionable.

To What Degree Does the Case of Denmark Give Evidence to Innovism as the Main Explanation for Prosperity as Observed in Modern Times

On a more general level, it seems Denmark is a good case for innovism. It was not capital—neither, land, money, machines, or human, that explain the impressive prosperity creation and wealth dissemination seen in Denmark in the twentieth century. While institutions were generally stable and trustworthy, they also changed fundamentally in the period, and they are not the key variable either. In fact, the causality goes the other way, institutional logics could change because of wealth creation. Further, the long focus on freedom of expression and freedom to trade is a key ingredients in innovism too. One challenge to innovism from the Danish case is the norm of trust. Good ideas should benefit from high levels of trust, but in a firm economy, where hierarchies often entail permission culture that also hampers innovation.

Index

© The Editor(s) (if applicable) and The Author(s), under exclusive license to Springer Nature Switzerland AG 2022
S. K. Sløk-Madsen, *Danish Capitalism in the 20th Century*, Palgrave Studies in Economic History,
https://doi.org/10.1007/978-3-031-04267-6

The manufacturer's authorised representative in the EU is Springer Nature Customer Service Centre GmbH, Europaplatz 3, 69115 Heidelberg, Germany. If you have any concerns regarding our products, please contact ProductSafety@springernature.com

Printed and bound by CPI Group (UK) Ltd, Croydon, CR0 4YY
28/09/2026
02224074-0002